Wonderful, Wearable Wire

Elegant and Easy Wire Jewelry Designs Using
the *Olympus WigJig*

Over 180 Designs for Beginning to
Advanced Wire Workers

Designs by
Karen Ray and Betty Bacon

Contributions from
Marjorie Helwig and Gary Helwig

Photography by Marilyn Gaizband and Sam Schaen

Helwig Industries, PO Box 5306, Arlington, VA 22205
800-579-WIRE -- 703-536-3690 (fax) -- sales@wigjig.com -- www.wigjig.com

ISBN 0-9650784-2-6

(Page intentionally left blank)

The Designers

Karen Ray holds a B.S. in mechanical engineering from Cornell University and an M.S. in management from Georgia Tech. She has worked in the government research and development community for 15 years, and is currently working for the U.S. Navy in Washington, D.C.

In the last few years, Karen rekindled her interest in jewelry making, as an artistic outlet, and owes all of her experience in wire working to Marj Helwig, who patiently inspired and encouraged her many students. Karen specializes in a wide variety of wire working designs, ranging from "miniature" (see *"Tiny Single Wrap Earrings,"* and *"Four Peg Chains"*) to "oversized" (see her chapter entitled *"Sun Catchers & Holiday Ornaments"*). Her relatives and friends count themselves blessed on holidays and birthdays since they benefit from Karen's love of wire working and jewelry making. In addition to showing and selling her jewelry in Northern Virginia, Karen has also had her wire and bead jewelry designs featured in Jewelry Craft magazine.

Betty Bacon has her roots in the South, though she has lived and worked in Northern Virginia since college. Her formal education was at Tennessee Wesleyan College, which prepared her to be a writer and teacher. She was lured to Washington, DC early in her career to work for the FBI. During this time, she did further study in art at American University. Eventually, while raising a son and two daughters, she became intrigued by real estate, and has been a partner in a successful firm for over 25 years.

Over the past six years, Betty found an equally consuming interest in the wire jewelry field. She initially studied with Marj Helwig, who was her mentor as well as her inspiration. Since then, she has studied under several other professional artists and her designs have been featured in "How to Make Your Own Great Earrings" by Jane La Ferla. Through her company, "Treasured Designs," Betty shows and sells her jewelry nationwide, including Hawaii. She also enjoys teaching a wide variety of wire working classes throughout the East.

Contributors

Marilyn Gaizband and *Sam Schaen* have been involved in photography since 1983. Since Marilyn began her jewelry business, Jigsaw Glass, four years ago, they have been concentrating on photographing various types of jewelry and glass beads. Examples of Marilyn's work can be found at www.jigsawglass.com. We thank Marilyn & Sam enormously for their contributions to the photography found in this book.

We also wish to thank *Bonnie Mason*, Managing Editor of "Rock & Gem" magazine, for her expertise in the technical editing of this book.

Marj and *Gary Helwig* designed several earring pieces for inclusion in this book. *Marj Helwig* provided inputs for the *"Wire Working Tips & Hints"* chapter. *Glenn Helwig*, *Karen Ray* and *Suzanne Helwig* provided editorial guidance and assistance.

(Page intentionally left blank)

 *This book is dedicated in memory of Marjorie Helwig*

In 1995, Marjorie Helwig published her first book, *"The Wonder of Wire,"* consisting of wire working designs for the *Original WigJig*. The tremendous response to this book launched her *WigJig* wire working business, and was the genesis of two dreams: the release of the *Olympus WigJig* as the world's first transparent jig, and the publishing of a book of *Olympus WigJig* designs — all for the students she loved to teach. Unfortunately, before she could make these dreams come true, she was diagnosed with cancer. After a very graceful and dignified farewell, she passed away in December of 1997.

This book is dedicated to Marj in the fulfillment of her dream. The support from her friends and family has been enormous: the designing by Karen and Betty, the photography by Marilyn and Sam, the design contributions from her son, Gary, and the editorial contributions from Bonnie, Karen, and Glenn, her husband. All of us are deeply indebted to Marj for the tremendous difference she has made in our lives through her love of wire, of the *Olympus WigJig*, and of us.

Perhaps the most meaningful way we can express our gratitude, as well as our loss, is through the words of Marj's granddaughter, Brittany. After saying good-bye to her grandmother, Brittany went home to Maine to write the poem on the following page.

Suzanne Helwig
October 1998

Designed for Marj
by Karen Ray

I went down to the shore today . . .

I went down to the shore today.
That's what I thought to do.
I sat right near the water,
And shed a tear for you.

I know you loved the ocean.
I remember walking there,
With you beside my shoulder,
We didn't have a care.

It seems like that was yesterday.
I really never knew,
That I'd cherish one small moment,
And all the others, too.

To let you go would be so hard.
So I dismissed the thought.
And I had to watch you struggle,
So I know how hard you fought.

When it was time for you to leave,
I didn't have such trouble.
You were like a different person.
But now the pain is double.

I try to think of memories
That wouldn't make me sore.
But I was wrong, they make no sense,
To know there won't be more.

How come you've left? I do not know.
But I don't ask why.
All I know is that I love you,
And that you had to die.

For my whole life I always knew,
That you were always there.
And now you're gone. See how it's hard?
It doesn't seem so fair.

When I need strength, I look to God,
And try to say that I'm
Still loving you from way down here,
But He's got perfect time.

I know you're watching down on me,
So I want you to hear,
That your family's all O.K. on Earth.
We know you're always near.

I know you always love me.
You know I love you too.
I went down to the shore today,
And shed a tear for you.

Brittany Wiggins
January 1998
(Age 13)

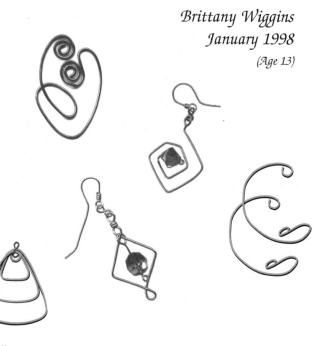

ii

Table of Contents

Table of Contents (Continued)

Table of Contents (Continued)

Table of Contents (Continued)

How

to

Use This Book

WigJig Olympus   Patent Pending

start

(Page intentionally left blank)

How to Use This Book

WigJig Olympus   Patent Pending

The best advice we can give you about using our book for wire working on the *Olympus WigJig* is to practice, practice, and practice some more. You will be surprised at how quickly you will master the basic techniques after wrapping several wire designs. The following outlines some key points to consider as you learn to wire work.

Peg Placement

The dark circles on the template indicate the exact location for placing the pegs into the holes of the *Olympus WigJig*. For the designs in this book, you should always use the jig template at the top of the page for placing the pegs into the jig. Align the jig on top of the design template until the holes are directly over the lightly-shaded circles, and place the pegs in the holes indicated by the dark circles. For creating your own designs, a blank template is provided at the end of this chapter.

Important: Each design includes a diagram showing the pegs placed within the wire piece, as well as directional arrows for making the design. The pegs included in this diagram have been adjusted slightly, and will not exactly match the pegs on the jig template. Therefore, when placing the pegs into the *Olympus WigJig*, please use the pegs that are shown on the template itself, located at the top of each design page.

Numbered Arrows & Design Sizes

Each design page includes an actual wire piece with numbered arrows indicating both the wrapping direction and the wrapping order. When making the design, wrap the wire around each peg in the direction of the arrows, noting whether the wrap is outside, inside, or completely around each peg. Also, a picture of the finished piece is provided for each design. If the picture has been enlarged (to show detail) or reduced in size, it has been noted as such.

Peg Sizes

The jig is packaged with two sizes of pegs. The longer pegs provide more space to hold the wire when wrapping multiple times around a single peg. Otherwise, both peg sizes can be used interchangeably.

How to Use This Book

WigJig Olympus   Patent Pending

(Continued)

Nylon Spacers

Several of the designs refer to the use of "nylon spacers." These are small plastic "donuts" that can be placed over the pegs to expand their size, resulting in loops and curves with larger diameters. Depending on the size of the inside diameter of the "donut hole," the nylon spacer can be placed on a single peg, on several adjacent pegs, or nested over another nylon spacer. An assortment of sizes of nylon spacers can be purchased at stores carrying the *Olympus WigJig* (check our web site at www.wigjig.com) or at most hardware stores.

Shape Retention

Some designs may require that the wire be flattened with a dowel or round nose pliers prior to removal from the jig. We have included a specific reference to this requirement in the directions when this step is mandatory. Additionally, some manipulation of the wire piece may be needed after removal from the jig to achieve the desired results. Wire hardening is also important for shape retention, and is discussed in detail in the *"Wire Working Tips & Hints"* chapter.

Wire Lengths

Wire lengths provided in the design directions are estimates only. Each wire worker varies in technique, so an exact length for each design cannot be specified. Before using expensive wire (sterling silver or gold–filled), we suggest that you make several samples from less-expensive wire, such as copper, documenting the length for your records. This will minimize, or eliminate, unnecessary waste of wire for your finished jewelry pieces. Generally, the smaller the gauge of wire (thicker in diameter), the longer the length of wire required to make the design. In other words, the same design will require more 16 gauge wire than 18 gauge wire.

Wrapping Techniques

To achieve a more rounded look, wrap the wire loosely around each peg. Holding the wire several inches away from the bend helps many wire workers achieve a softer, rounder look.

To achieve a sharper and more angular look, wrap tightly around each peg by holding your fingers close to the pegs. Some wire workers find that wrapping in one specific direction

How to Use This Book

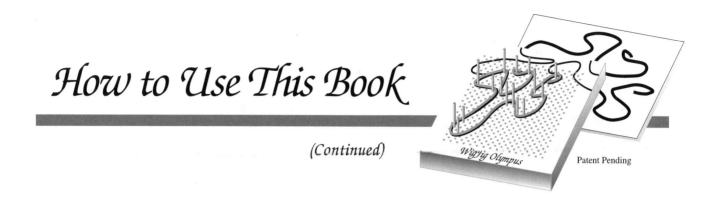

(Continued)

WigJig Olympus   Patent Pending

results in a tighter or looser look, depending on individual technique.

For many *Olympus WigJig* users, turning the jig while holding the wire stationary produces better control and results. Again, wire wrapping techniques are different for each wire worker, and experimentation and practice will determine the best method for you.

Starting Techniques: Up the Wire, Down the Wire, Eye Loops, Center of the Wire

How you place your wire on the *Olympus WigJig* to start wrapping the design is very important. There are three basic ways to start the designs in this book:

- Starting Loop, (up the wire or down the wire)
- Eye Loop
- Starting in the Center (up the wire or down the wire)

Because an integral part of the design rests with the starting technique, we have provided detailed directions for each of these three methods in the chapter *"Wire Working Tips & Hints"* (see the sections entitled *"How to Make a Starting Loop," "How to Make an Eye Loop,"* and *"How to Start at the Center of the Wire"*).

Finishing Techniques

There are a variety of finishing techniques that can be used to complete your wire designs. In some cases, the final wrap on the jig will serve as the only finishing required (other than cutting the wire tail). For other designs, wrapping the wire tail around another part of the piece, usually the neck of the starting loop, will finish the piece. In some cases, tucking the final ending loop behind the starting loop will lock the design into place. Our instructions include appropriate finishing techniques for each design.

Work Habits

Safe work habits are important when working with wire. When cutting, avoid injury from flying pieces of wire by cupping one hand over the wire as you cut, or by pointing the work into a waste container. Additionally, safety glasses are a must, particularly if there are two or more people working in the same area.

How to Use This Book

WigJig Olympus   Patent Pending

(Continued)

Another important work habit to develop involves elimination of stress to the wrist, by limiting the range of movement. A turning motion to the right should be balanced by one to the left. For example, as you are coiling or turning a segment of wire gripped in your pliers, it is best make the coils/turns in small segments by rotating the wrist slightly in one direction, releasing the grip on the wire, and slipping the pliers back in the opposite direction before continuing the rotation. This will help prevent fatigue and/or injury to the wrist from overuse.

Uniformity

Uniformity – the classic sign of a professional wire worker – is clearly an important skill to develop. Remember to keep the wire consistently placed at the same point in the nose of the pliers so that the loops are of uniform size. In the beginning, it helps to mark the nose of the pliers with a permanent marker to assist you in finding this spot on the pliers repeatedly.

Designing

The sky is the limit for new ideas and designs on the *Olympus WigJig*. For your convenience, we have placed a template at the end of this chapter to copy for your designs. Please note the special copying instructions at the bottom of the page.

Wire Working Tips

In addition to designing on the jig, there are several key wire working techniques that must be mastered to ensure your finished jewelry pieces are professional in workmanship and quality. We have compiled a section of "how to" instructions in the *"Wire Working Tips & Hints"* chapter. This chapter discusses how to buy tools and supplies, how to choose wire, how to wrap beads, how to make pins, coils, scrolls, cages, and much more. Regardless of experience level, we think you will find these tips to be invaluable. As you use the book, if you find a technique with which you are unfamiliar, we suggest you review the *"Wire Working Tips & Hints"* chapter for additional information.

How to Use This Book

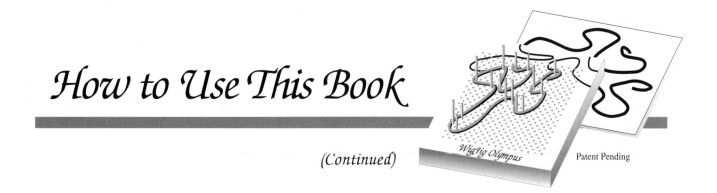

(Continued)

WigJig Olympus

Patent Pending

Photography

We recommend you review the photos in the book closely as you begin using the *Olympus WigJig*. These jewelry, holiday and ornamental pieces provide numerous examples of wire working techniques, designs, wire types and wire color. These photos prove that the number of designs that can be made on the *Olympus WigJig* is endless. The only limitation is your imagination.

Happy designing! We hope you enjoy reading and using *"Wonderful, Wearable Wire"* as much as we have enjoyed designing, writing, and publishing this book.

P.S. If you have questions or suggestions for future editions of this book, please feel free to write (PO Box 5306, Arlington, VA 22205), phone (800-579-WIRE), fax (703-536-3690) or email (sales@wigjig.com).

Olympus WigJig Template

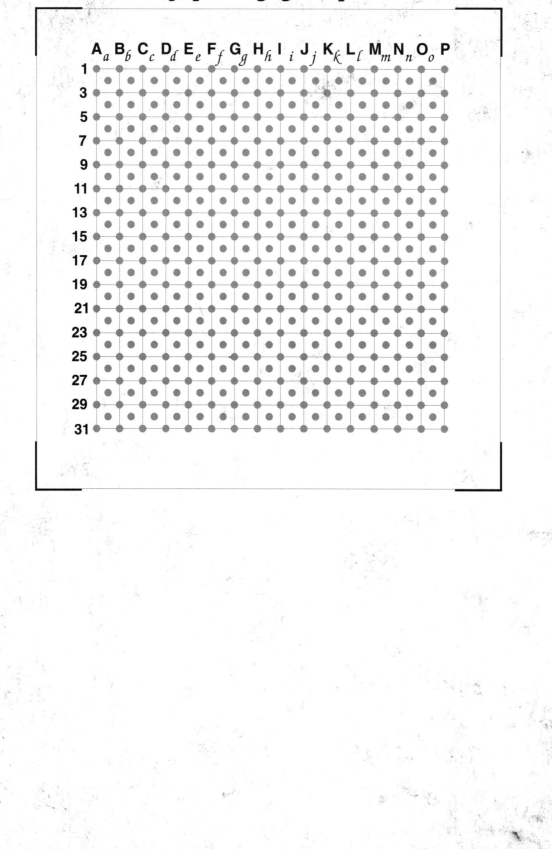

Chains, Links
and
Clasps

Wire designs in photograph on reverse side: Loopy Collaboration (pg. 19), Celtic Knot Links (pg. 22), Helwig Classic (pg. 23), Five Petals (pg. 26), Modern Curve (pg. 30), Infinity Link (pg. 34), Zigs & Zags (pg. 42), Frog Yoke (pg. 119).

WigJig Olympus Template

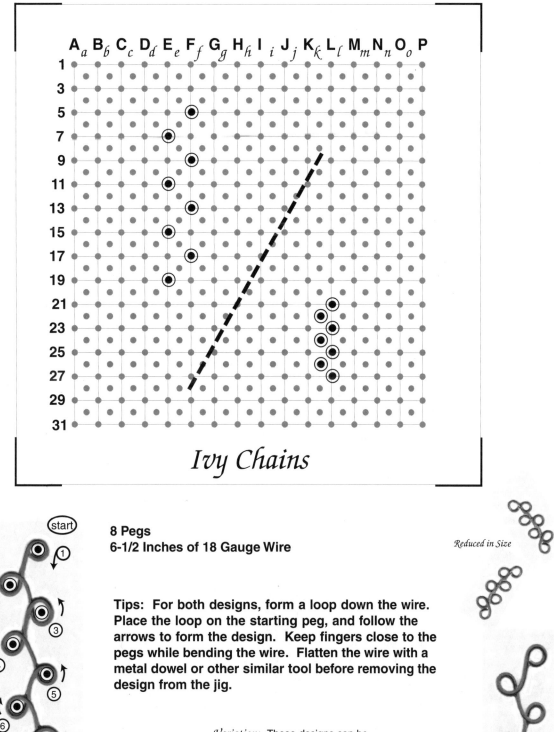

A a B b C c D d E e F f G g H h I i J j K k L l M m N n O o P

1 3 5 7 9 11 13 15 17 19 21 23 25 27 29 31

Ivy Chains

start

1
2
3
4
5
6
7
8

Enlarged to Show Detail

8 Pegs
6-1/2 Inches of 18 Gauge Wire

Tips: For both designs, form a loop down the wire. Place the loop on the starting peg, and follow the arrows to form the design. Keep fingers close to the pegs while bending the wire. Flatten the wire with a metal dowel or other similar tool before removing the design from the jig.

Variation: These designs can be varied by altering the number of pegs and the wire length to achieve different effects.

7 Pegs
5 Inches of 20 Gauge Wire

Reduced in Size

WigJig Olympus Template

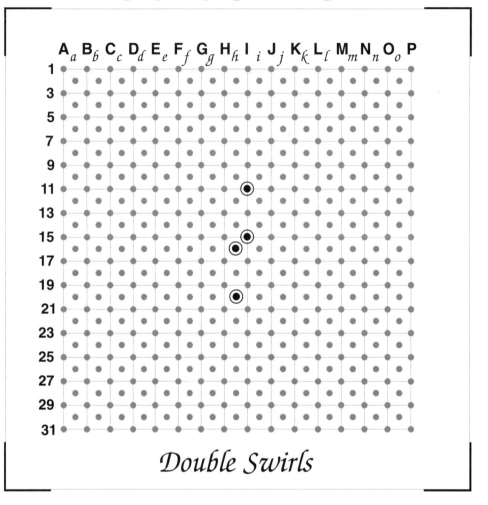

Double Swirls

4 Pegs
4 to 6 Inches of 18 Gauge Wire, based on size of coils/scrolls
5 to 7 Inches of 16 Gauge Wire, based on size of coils/scrolls

Reduced in Size

Tips: Measure, then place the center of the wire between the two center pegs, with the natural curve of the wire following the curve of the first wrap (down the wire). Bend the right tail up and around the top peg. Bend the left tail down and around the bottom peg. Remove the wire design from the jig and form coils or scrolls at each end.

For tips on making scrolls and coils, see *"How to Make a Coil or Scroll"* in the *"Wire Working Tips & Hints"* chapter.

For tips on starting a design in the center of the wire, see *"How to Start at the Center of the Wire"* in the *"Wire Working Tips & Hints"* chapter.

Variation: The designs above show a variety of pieces that can be made using this peg placement. For designs incorporating a bead, thread the bead onto the center of the wire, bend one side of the wire up and the other wire down. Remove the two center pegs on the jig, and place the bead at the location of the removed pegs. Hold the bead in place manually, and follow the arrows to complete the design.

Note: Pegs placed inside the wire design(s) on this page have been slightly adjusted for illustrative purposes. Please copy the peg placements on the jig template when making the design(s).

WigJig Olympus Template

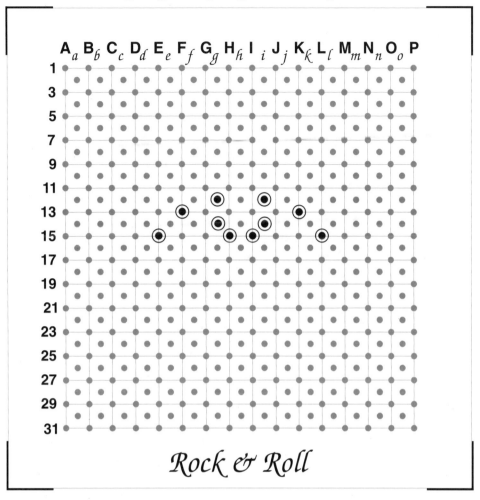

Row labels (left): 1, 3, 5, 7, 9, 11, 13, 15, 17, 19, 21, 23, 25, 27, 29, 31

Column labels (top): A a B b C c D d E e F f G g H h I i J j K k L l M m N n O o P

Rock & Roll

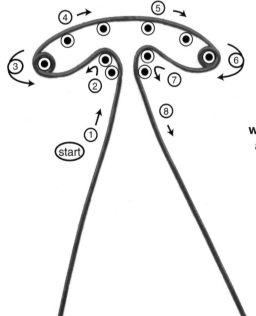

10 Pegs
15 Inches of 16 Gauge Wire

Tips: Measure 3-1/2 inches from one end. Place this point at the starting peg, letting the natural curve of the wire follow the curve of the first wrap (down the wire). Follow the arrows to form the design. Remove the piece from the jig.

Trim both wire tails 3 inches from the first and last curves that were wrapped. Form a coil at each end.

Reduced in Size

Variation (not shown): After completing the wrap at Arrow 3, beads may be threaded onto the wire (Arrows 4 and 5) before starting the wrap at Arrow 6.

For tips on making scrolls and coils, see *"How to Make a Coil or Scroll"* in the *"Wire Working Tips & Hints"* chapter.

Note: Pegs placed inside the wire design(s) on this page have been slightly adjusted for illustrative purposes. Please copy the peg placements on the jig template when making the design(s).

WigJig Olympus Template

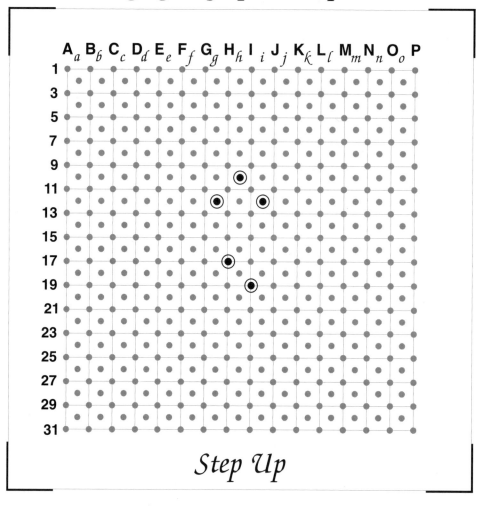

Step Up

5 Pegs
5 Inches of 18 Gauge Wire

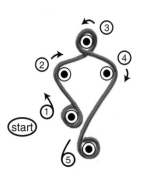

Tips: Form a loop down the wire. Place the loop on the starting peg, and follow the arrows to form the design.

WigJig Olympus Template

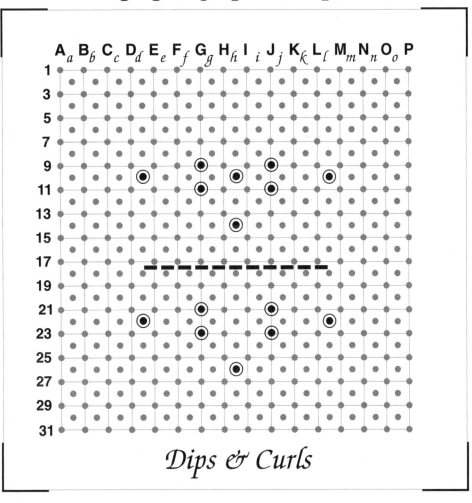

A_a B_b C_c D_d E_e F_f G_g H_h I_i J_j K_k L_l M_m N_n O_o P

Dips & Curls

8 Pegs
10 Inches of 16 Gauge Wire

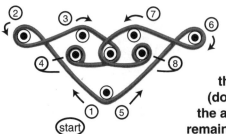

Tips: Measure, then place the center of the wire on the lowest peg, letting the natural curve of the wire follow the curve of the first wrap of the design (down the wire). Wrap one wire tail, following the arrows. Complete the design by wrapping the remaining wire tail.

Reduced in Size

7 Pegs
10 Inches of 16 Gauge Wire

Reduced in Size

Variation: This variation is formed by removing the center peg (as shown on the lower half of the jig template).

For tips on starting a design in the center of the wire, see *"How to Start at the Center of the Wire"* in the *"Wire Working Tips & Hints"* chapter.

WigJig Olympus Template

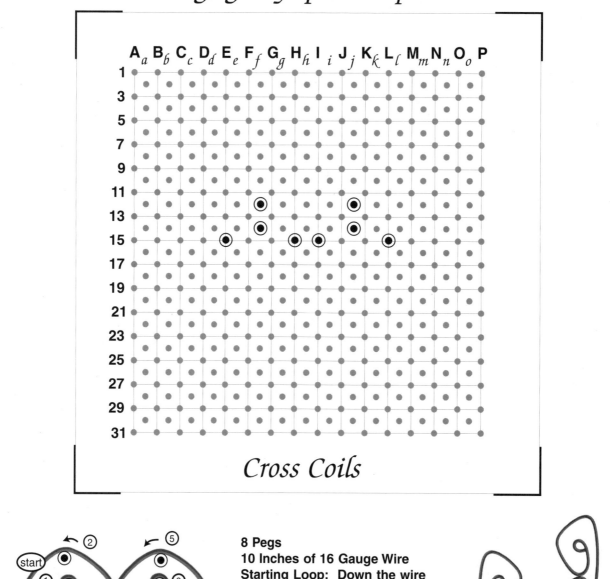

A a B b C c D d E e F f G g H h I i J j K k L l M m N n O o P

1
3
5
7
9
11
13
15
17
19
21
23
25
27
29
31

Cross Coils

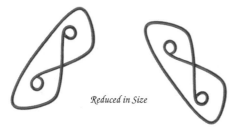

8 Pegs
10 Inches of 16 Gauge Wire
Starting Loop: Down the wire

Reduced in Size

Tips: Form a starting loop up or down the wire, as indicated for each design. Place the loop on the starting peg, and follow the arrows to complete the design.

Reduced in Size

8 Pegs
10 Inches of 16 Gauge Wire
Starting Loop: Up the wire

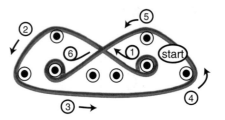

Note: Pegs placed inside the wire design(s) on this page have been slightly adjusted for illustrative purposes. Please copy the peg placements on the jig template when making the design(s).

© 1998, Helwig Industries, LLC
& Betty Bacon

16

WigJig Olympus™ Template

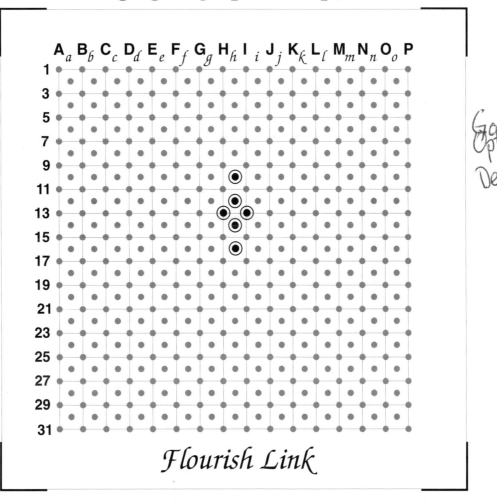

```
      A a B b C c D d E e F f G g H h I i J j K k L l M m N n O o P
  1
  3
  5
  7
  9
 11
 13
 15
 17
 19
 21
 23
 25
 27
 29
 31
```

Good Option: Delete 12H and 14H

Flourish Link

6 Pegs
3 Inches of 18 Gauge Wire

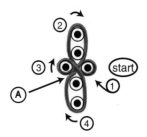

Tips: Form a loop down the wire. Place the loop on the starting peg, and follow the arrows to form the design. Keep fingers close to the pegs while bending the wire. Flatten the wire with a metal dowel or other similar tool before removing the design from the jig. Clip tail at Arrow A.

6 Pegs
5 Inches of 18 Gauge Wire

Variation: This filigree variation is formed by starting and ending at the top peg, and by wrapping completely around the bottom peg.

Note: Pegs placed inside the wire design(s) on this page have been slightly adjusted for illustrative purposes. Please copy the peg placements on the jig template when making the design(s).

WigJig Olympus Template

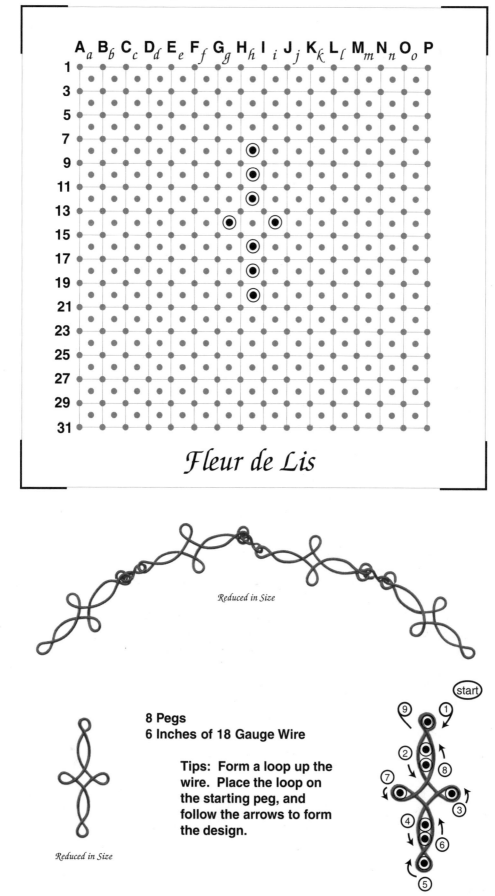

Fleur de Lis

Reduced in Size

Reduced in Size

8 Pegs
6 Inches of 18 Gauge Wire

Tips: Form a loop up the wire. Place the loop on the starting peg, and follow the arrows to form the design.

start

WigJig Olympus Template

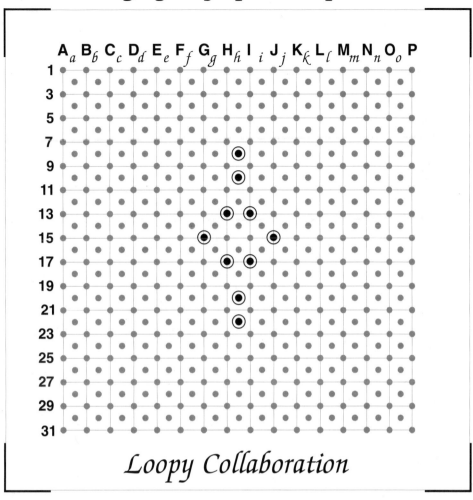

A a B b C c D d E e F f G g H h I i J j K k L l M m N n O o P

1 3 5 7 9 11 13 15 17 19 21 23 25 27 29 31

Loopy Collaboration

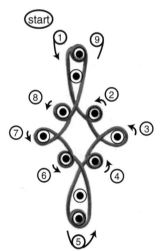

10 Pegs
10 Inches of 18 Gauge Wire

Tips: Form a loop down the wire.
Place the loop on the starting peg, and
follow the arrows to form the design.

Note: Pegs placed inside the wire design(s) on this
page have been slightly adjusted for illustrative
purposes. Please copy the peg placements on the jig
template when making the design(s).

19

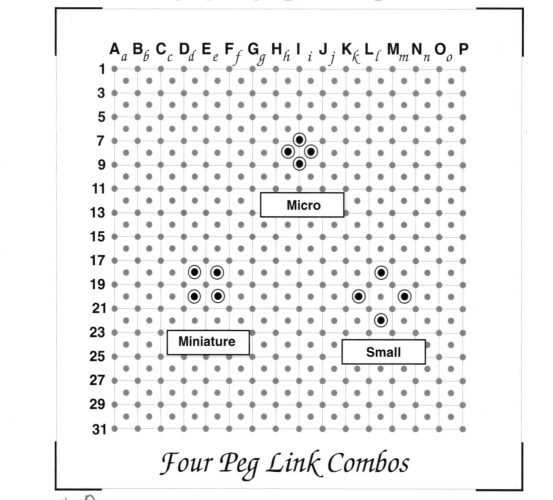

4 Pegs *Mini 3" -20*
3 Inches of 18 Gauge Wire (Micro)
Starting Loop: Down the wire

Note: Wire lengths are provided for Micro size links.

4 Pegs
4 Inches of 18 Gauge Wire
Starting Loop: Up the wire

Tips: Form a loop up or down the wire, as indicated for each design. Place the loop on the starting peg, and follow the arrows to form the design. Keep fingers close to the pegs while bending the wire. Flatten the wire with a metal dowel or other similar tool before removing the design from the jig. For the Micro size links, 20 gauge wire can also be used.

Enlarged to Show Detail

Enlarged to Show Detail

Note: Pegs placed inside the wire design(s) on this page have been slightly adjusted for illustrative purposes. Please copy the peg placements on the jig template when making the design(s).

WigJig Olympus Template

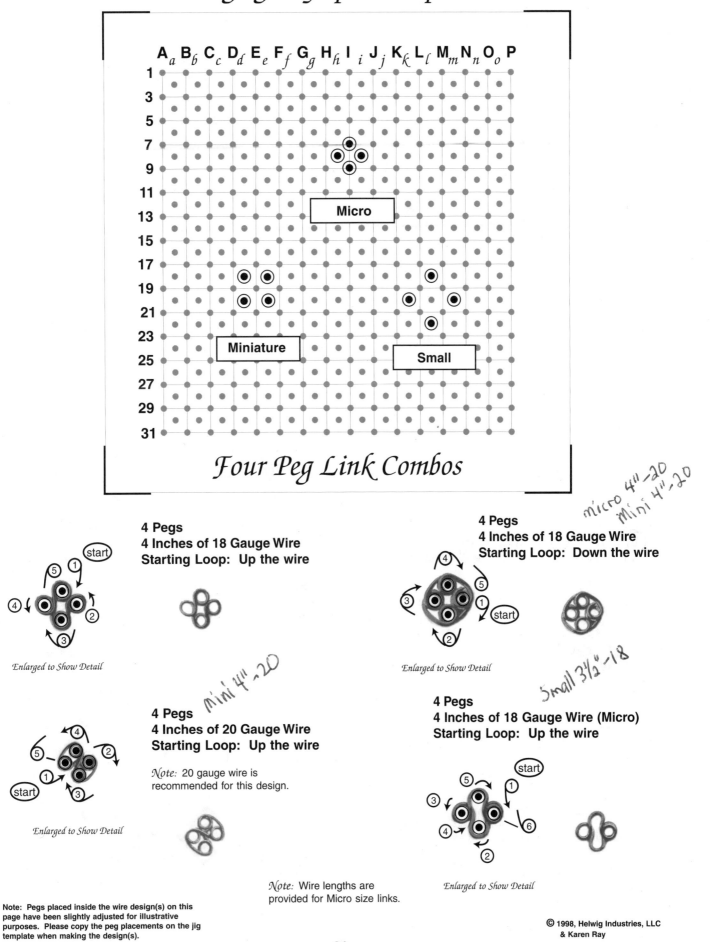

A_a **B**_b **C**_c **D**_d **E**_e **F**_f **G**_g **H**_h **I**_i **J**_j **K**_k **L**_l **M**_m **N**_n **O**_o **P**

Micro

Miniature

Small

Four Peg Link Combos

4 Pegs
4 Inches of 18 Gauge Wire
Starting Loop: Up the wire

Enlarged to Show Detail

4 Pegs
4 Inches of 18 Gauge Wire
Starting Loop: Down the wire

Enlarged to Show Detail

micro 4"-20
Mini 4"-20

4 Pegs
4 Inches of 20 Gauge Wire
Starting Loop: Up the wire

Note: 20 gauge wire is
recommended for this design.

Mini 4"-20

4 Pegs
4 Inches of 18 Gauge Wire (Micro)
Starting Loop: Up the wire

Small 3½"-18

Enlarged to Show Detail

Note: Wire lengths are
provided for Micro size links.

Enlarged to Show Detail

Note: Pegs placed inside the wire design(s) on this
page have been slightly adjusted for illustrative
purposes. Please copy the peg placements on the jig
template when making the design(s).

WigJig Olympus Template

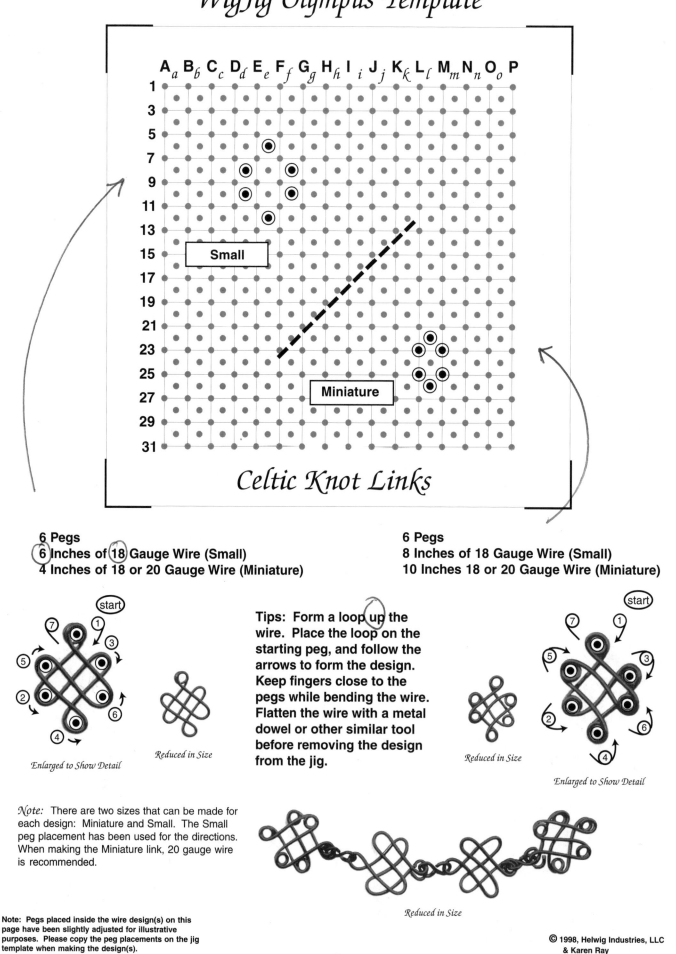

A_a B_b C_c D_d E_e F_f G_g H_h I_i J_j K_k L_l M_m N_n O_o P

Small

Miniature

Celtic Knot Links

6 Pegs
6 Inches of 18 Gauge Wire (Small)
4 Inches of 18 or 20 Gauge Wire (Miniature)

6 Pegs
8 Inches of 18 Gauge Wire (Small)
10 Inches 18 or 20 Gauge Wire (Miniature)

start

7 1
3
5
2
6
4

Enlarged to Show Detail

Reduced in Size

Tips: Form a loop up the wire. Place the loop on the starting peg, and follow the arrows to form the design. Keep fingers close to the pegs while bending the wire. Flatten the wire with a metal dowel or other similar tool before removing the design from the jig.

start

7 1
5 3
2 6
4

Reduced in Size

Enlarged to Show Detail

Note: There are two sizes that can be made for each design: Miniature and Small. The Small peg placement has been used for the directions. When making the Miniature link, 20 gauge wire is recommended.

Reduced in Size

Note: Pegs placed inside the wire design(s) on this page have been slightly adjusted for illustrative purposes. Please copy the peg placements on the jig template when making the design(s).

WigJig Olympus Template

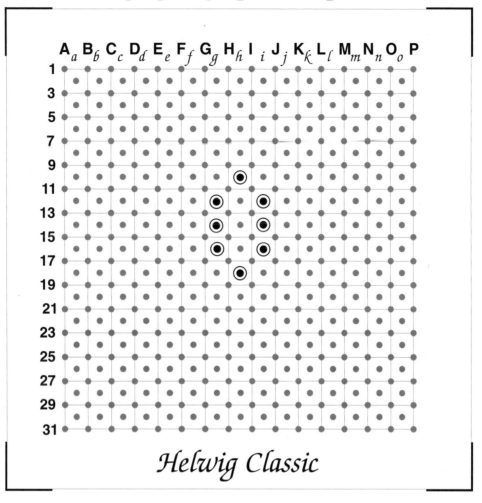

A_a B_b C_c D_d E_e F_f G_g H_h I_i J_j K_k L_l M_m N_n O_o P

Helwig Classic

8 Pegs
9 Inches of 18 Gauge Wire
10 Inches of 16 Gauge Wire

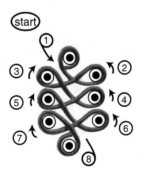

Tips: Form a loop down the wire. Place the loop on the starting peg, and follow the arrows to form the design.

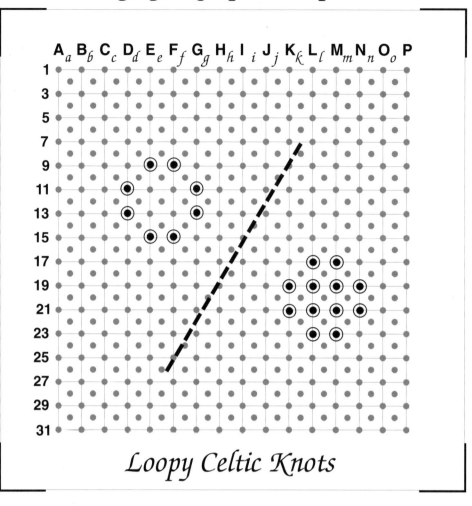

A$_a$ **B**$_b$ **C**$_c$ **D**$_d$ **E**$_e$ **F**$_f$ **G**$_g$ **H**$_h$ **I**$_i$ **J**$_j$ **K**$_k$ **L**$_l$ **M**$_m$ **N**$_n$ **O**$_o$ **P**

Loopy Celtic Knots

8 Pegs
6 Inches of 18 Gauge Wire

12 Pegs
6 Inches of 18 Gauge Wire

Clip wire tail here.

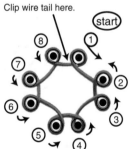

Tips: Form a loop down the wire. Place the loop on the starting peg, and follow the arrows to form the design. For the design to the left, clip the wire tail, as shown.

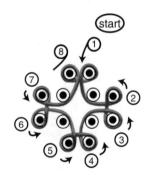

Reduced in Size

Note: Pegs placed inside the wire design(s) on this page have been slightly adjusted for illustrative purposes. Please copy the peg placements on the jig template when making the design(s).

24

WigJig Olympus Template

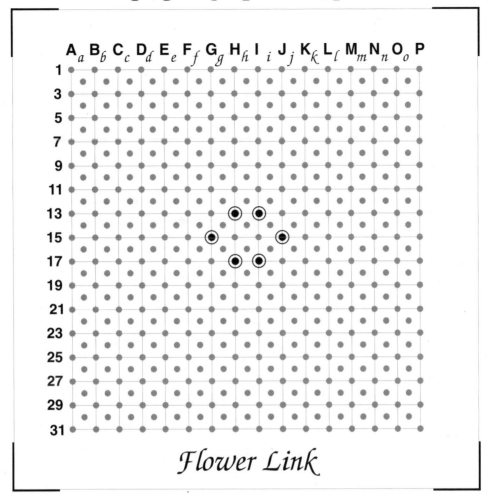

A a B b C c D d E e F f G g H h I i J j K k L l M m N n O o P

1 3 5 7 9 11 13 15 17 19 21 23 25 27 29 31

Flower Link

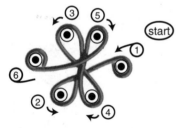

Enlarged to Show Detail

6 Pegs
6 Inches of 18 Gauge Wire

Tips: Form a loop
down the wire. Place
the loop on the starting
peg, and follow the
arrows to form the
design.

© 1998, Helwig Industries, LLC
& Karen Ray

WigJig Olympus Template

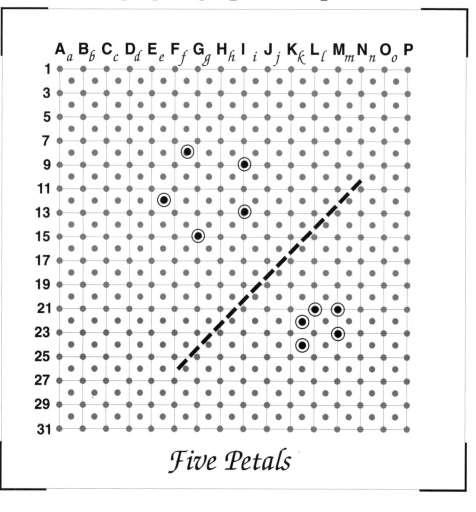

A B C D E F G H I J K L M N O P

1 3 5 7 9 11 13 15 17 19 21 23 25 27 29 31

Five Petals

5 Pegs
8-1/2 Inches of 18 Gauge Wire
9 Inches of 16 Gauge Wire

5 Pegs
3 Inches of 18 Gauge Wire

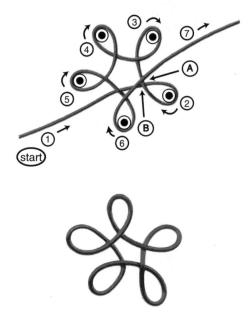

Tips: Starting 1-1/2 inches from the end of the wire, place the wire on the starting peg (Arrow 2) with the natural curve of the wire in the same direction as the first wrap (down the wire). Follow the arrows to form the design. Remove the piece from the jig.

On the larger design, the wire tails will meet at the base of the last petal formed. Cut the wire tails at Arrows A and B.

For the smaller design, press the wire with fingers into a flower shape as shown in the finished design. Cut both wire tails at the base of the petal (Arrows C and D).

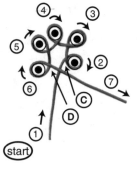

For tips on starting a design in the center of the wire, see *"How to Start at the Center of the Wire"* in the *"Wire Working Tips & Hints"* chapter.

Note: Pegs placed inside the wire design(s) on this page have been slightly adjusted for illustrative purposes. Please copy the peg placements on the jig template when making the design(s).

WigJig Olympus Template

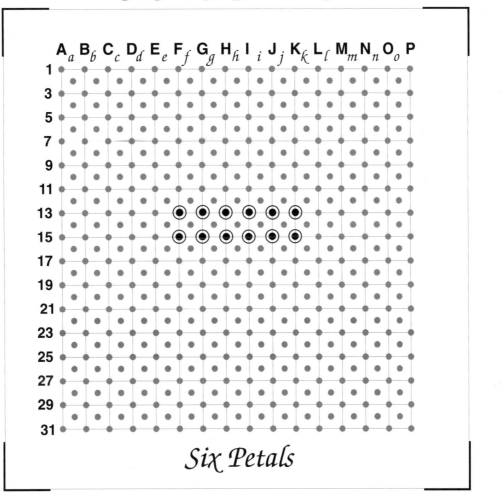

Six Petals

Tips: Leaving a 1 inch wire tail, place the wire under the starting peg, allowing the natural curve of the wire to follow the curve of the first wrap (down the wire). Follow the arrows to form the design, wrapping tightly around each peg. Remove the wire piece from the jig.

Form the flower by bending the wire in a circle, as shown in the finished piece. Complete by cutting the wire tails so that the ends meet behind a top wire.

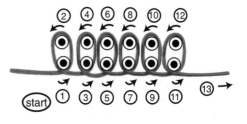

12 Pegs
10 Inches of 18 Gauge Wire

Note: A larger version of this design called *"Loops to Flowers"* can be found in the *"Pendants and Earrings"* chapter.

For tips on starting a design in the center of the wire, see *"How to Start at the Center of the Wire"* in the *"Wire Working Tips & Hints"* chapter.

WigJig Olympus Template

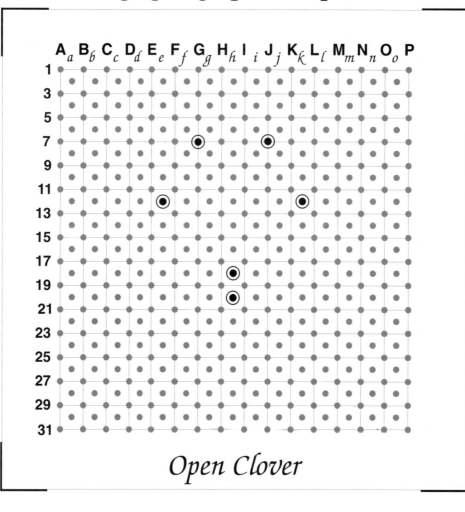

A_a B_b C_c D_d E_e F_f G_g H_h I_i J_j K_k L_l M_m N_n O_o P

Open Clover

6 Pegs
10 Inches of 16 Gauge Wire
10 Inches of 18 Gauge Wire

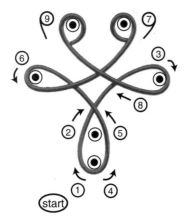

Tips: Measure, then place the center of the wire at the starting peg with the natural curve of the wire in the opposite direction of the curve of the first wrap (up the wire). Wrap the first wire tail through Arrow 3, then stop. Holding this wire tail in place, return to the starting peg and fully wrap the other wire tail through Arrow 7. Return to the first wire tail at Arrow 8, and complete the design.

For tips on starting a design in the center of the wire, see *"How to Start at the Center of the Wire"* in the *"Wire Working Tips & Hints"* chapter.

WigJig Olympus Template

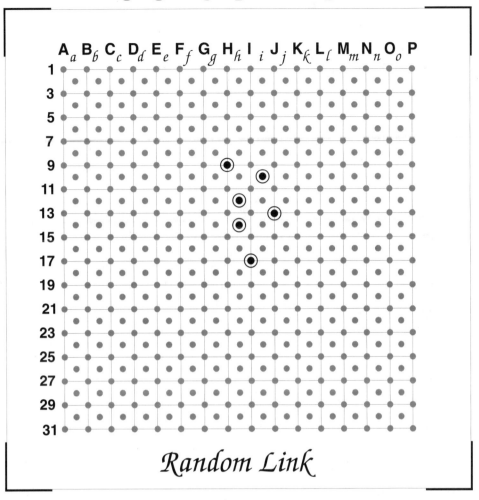

Random Link

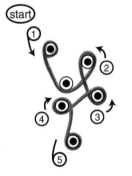

6 Pegs
5 Inches of 18 Gauge Wire

Tips: Form a loop down the wire. Place the loop on the starting peg, and follow the arrows to form the design. Keep fingers close to the pegs while bending the wire. Flatten the wire with a metal dowel or other similar tool before removing the design from the jig.

Reduced in Size

Note: Pegs placed inside the wire design(s) on this page have been slightly adjusted for illustrative purposes. Please copy the peg placements on the jig template when making the design(s).

© 1998, Helwig Industries, LLC
& Karen Ray

WigJig Olympus Template

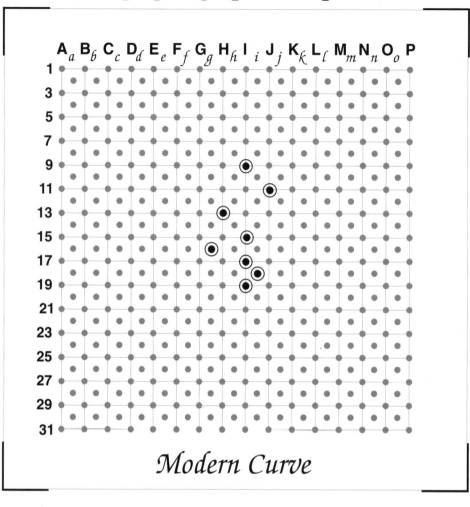

Modern Curve

Interim Piece

8 Pegs
8 Inches of 18 Gauge Wire
8-1/2 Inches of 16 Gauge Wire

Tips: Form a loop down the wire. Place the loop on the starting peg, and follow the arrows to form the design. Remove the piece from the jig and finish by gently bending the wire manually to place the ending loop inside the large bottom loop, as shown to the right.

WigJig Olympus Template

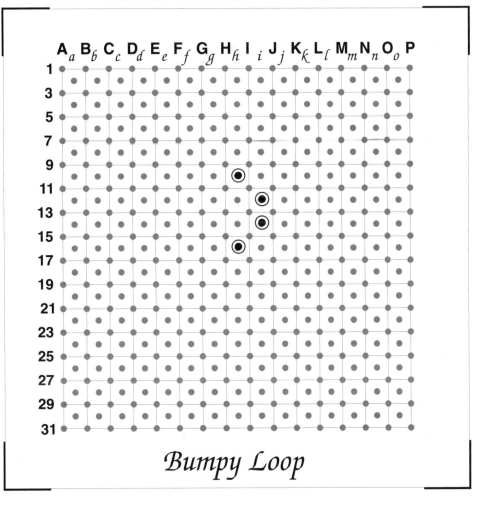

A_a B_b C_c D_d E_e F_f G_g H_h I_i J_j K_k L_l M_m N_n O_o P

Bumpy Loop

4 Pegs
8 Inches of 18 Gauge Wire

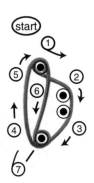

Tips: Form a loop up the wire. Place the loop on the starting peg, and follow the arrows to form the design.

WigJig Olympus Template

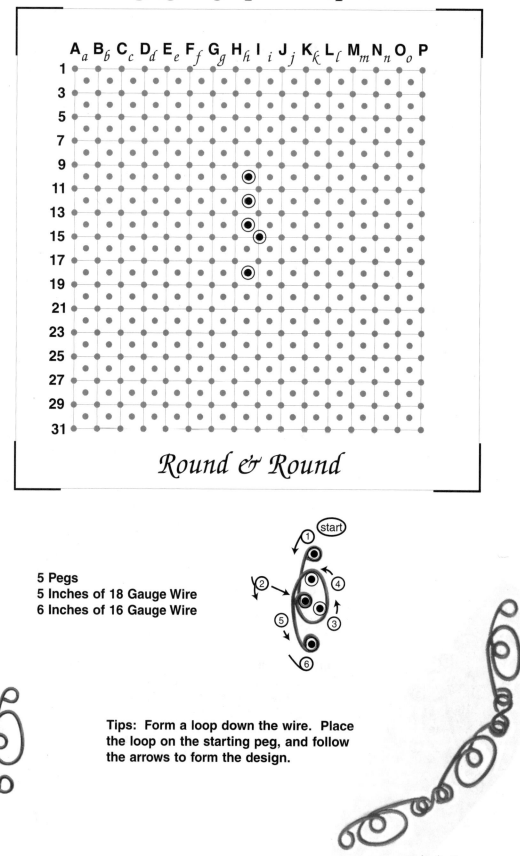

Round & Round

5 Pegs
5 Inches of 18 Gauge Wire
6 Inches of 16 Gauge Wire

Tips: Form a loop down the wire. Place the loop on the starting peg, and follow the arrows to form the design.

Reduced in Size

WigJig Olympus Template

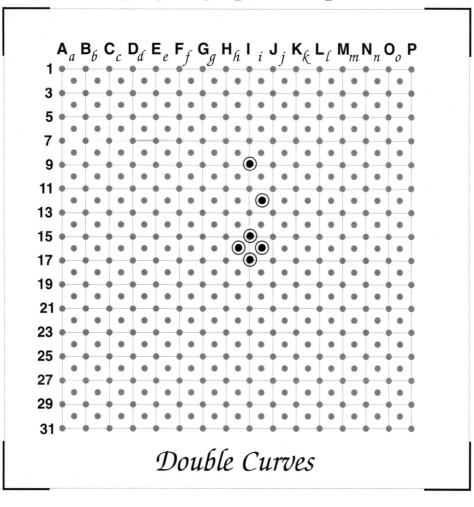

A a B b C c D d E e F f G g H h I i J j K k L l M m N n O o P

Double Curves

6 Pegs
5 Inches of 16 Gauge Wire

Tips: Form a loop down the wire. Place the loop on the starting peg, and follow the arrows to form the design.

WigJig Olympus Template

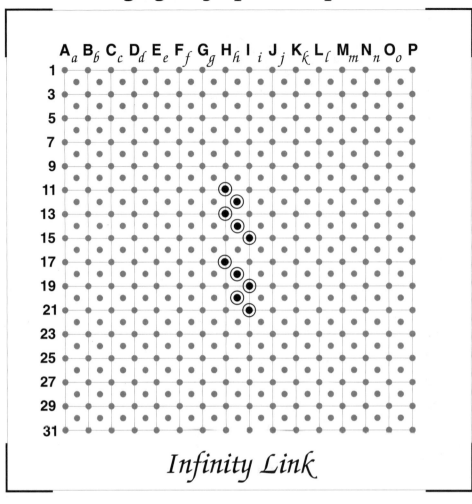

A_a B_b C_c D_d E_e F_f G_g H_h I_i J_j K_k L_l M_m N_n O_o P

Infinity Link

10 Pegs
5 Inches of 18 Gauge Wire

Tips: Form a loop down the wire. Place the loop on the starting peg, and follow the arrows to form the design.

Variation: The design to the right is a variation in which the beginning and ending loops have been cut away after removing the piece from the jig.

Reduced in Size

Note: Pegs placed inside the wire design(s) on this page have been slightly adjusted for illustrative purposes. Please copy the peg placements on the jig template when making the design(s).

34

WigJig Olympus Template

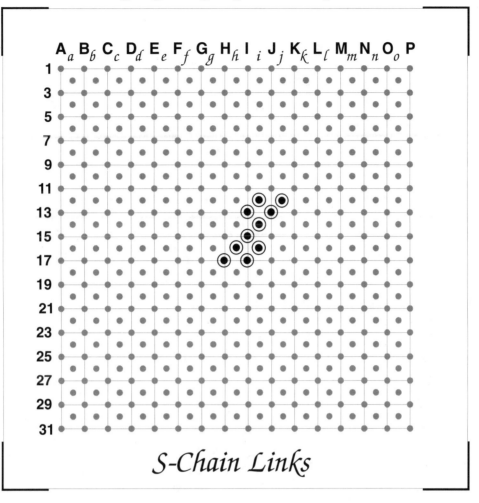

A_a B_b C_c D_d E_e F_f G_g H_h I_i J_j K_k L_l M_m N_n O_o P

S-Chain Links

10 Pegs
5 Inches of 18 Gauge Wire

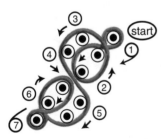

Enlarged to Show Detail

Tips: Form a loop up the wire. Place the loop on the starting peg, and follow the arrows to form the design. Keep fingers close to the pegs while bending the wire. Flatten the wire with a metal dowel or other similar tool before removing the design from the jig.

Variation: The design to the left is a variation in which the beginning and ending loops have been trimmed after removing the piece from the jig.

WigJig Olympus Template

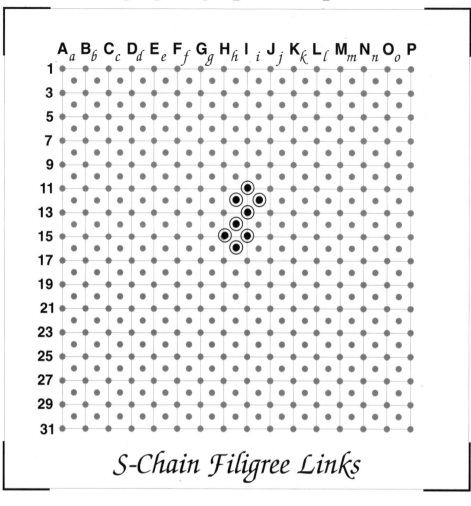

A_a B_b C_c D_d E_e F_f G_g H_h I_i J_j K_k L_l M_m N_n O_o P

1 3 5 7 9 11 13 15 17 19 21 23 25 27 29 31

S-Chain Filigree Links

8 Pegs
5 Inches of 18 Gauge Wire

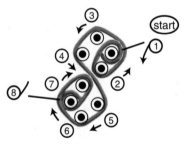

Enlarged to Show Detail

Tips: Form a loop down the wire. Place the loop on the starting peg, and follow the arrows to form the design. Keep fingers close to the pegs while bending the wire. Flatten the wire with a metal dowel or other similar tool before removing the design from the jig.

Variation: The design to the right is a variation in which the wire is wrapped loosely around the pegs, resulting in a more curved, and less angular link. This curved look is achieved by holding fingers away from the pegs when wrapping.

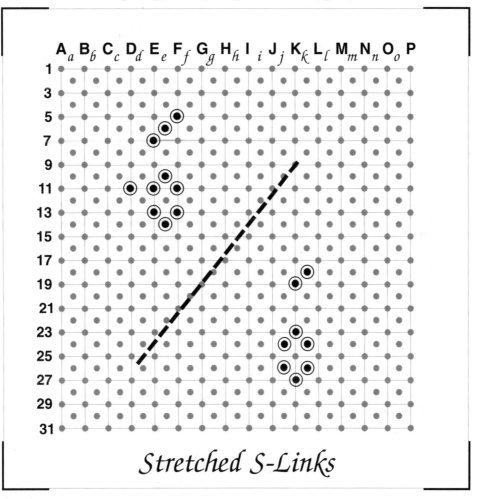

Stretched S-Links

10 Pegs
6 Inches of 18 Gauge Wire

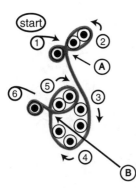

Tips: Form a loop up the wire. Place the loop on the starting peg, and follow the arrows to form the design. Remove the design from the jig, and cut away the beginning and ending loops (Arrows A and B) to finish.

8 Pegs
6 Inches of 18 Gauge Wire

Tips: Form a loop down the wire. Place the loop on the starting peg, and follow the arrows to form the design.

Note: Pegs placed inside the wire design(s) on this page have been slightly adjusted for illustrative purposes. Please copy the peg placements on the jig template when making the design(s).

WigJig Olympus Template

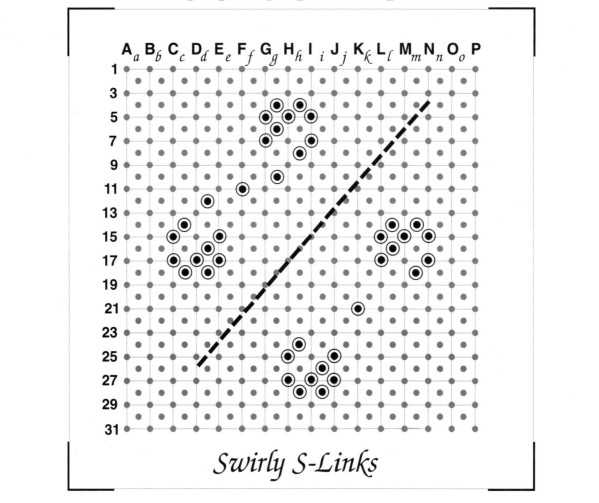

A$_a$ B$_b$ C$_c$ D$_d$ E$_e$ F$_f$ G$_g$ H$_h$ I$_i$ J$_j$ K$_k$ L$_l$ M$_m$ N$_n$ O$_o$ P

Swirly S-Links

Reduced in Size

21 Pegs
10 Inches of 18 Gauge Wire (Yoke)
13 Inches of 18 Gauge Wire (Pin)

Links: **Form a loop down the wire. Place the loop on the starting peg, and follow the arrows to form the design.**

Pin: **Form a double loop down the wire using the round nose pliers. Place both loops on the starting peg, and follow the arrows to form the design. Wrap the last peg twice to form another double loop. Remove the piece from the jig. To finish, follow the directions in** *"How to Make a Pin Using the Jig"* **in the** *"Wire Working Tips & Hints"* **chapter.**

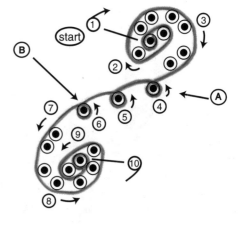

19 Pegs
9 Inches of 18 Gauge Wi

Reduced in Size

Variation: Form the design to the left by removing the two pegs marked A & B in the diagram above. The exact peg placement is shown on the template in the lower right corner.

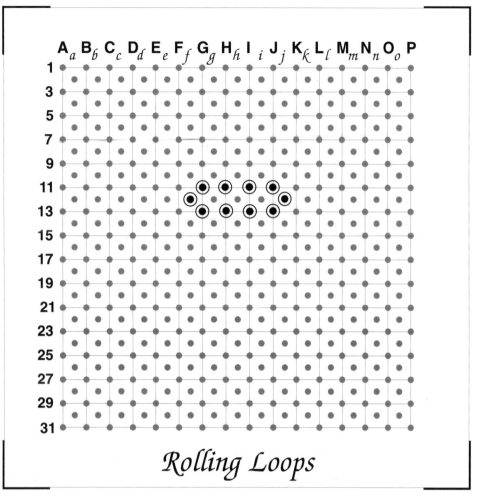

A _a B _b C _c D _d E _e F _f G _g H _h I _i J _j K _k L _l M _m N _n O _o P

Rolling Loops

10 Pegs
6 Inches of 18 Gauge Wire
8 Inches of 16 Gauge Wire

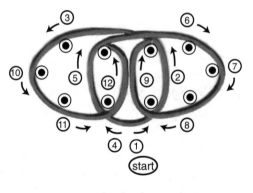

Enlarged to Show Detail

Tips: Measure, then place the center of the wire between the bottom two center pegs, letting the natural curve of the wire follow the curve of the first wrap (down the wire). Wrap the first wire tail through Arrow 3, then stop. Holding this wire tail in place, return to the starting pegs at Arrow 4, and fully wrap the other wire tail around all pegs, following the arrows. Then return to the first wire tail at Arrow 10 and complete its wrap. Clip wire tails as shown.

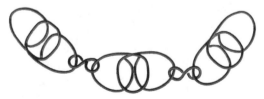

Reduced in Size

For tips on starting a design in the center of the wire, see *"How to Start at the Center of the Wire"* in the *"Wire Working Tips & Hints"* chapter.

Note: Pegs placed inside the wire design(s) on this page have been slightly adjusted for illustrative purposes. Please copy the peg placements on the jig template when making the design(s).

WigJig Olympus Template

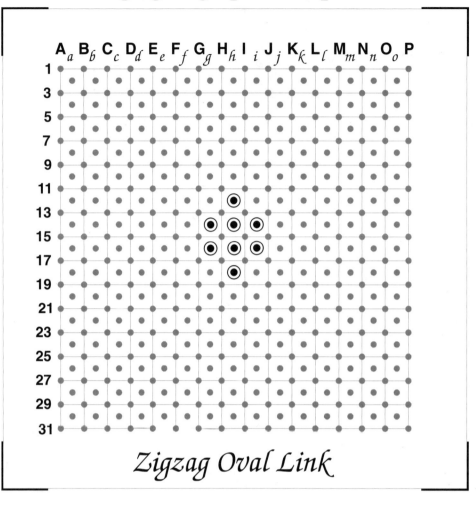

Zigzag Oval Link

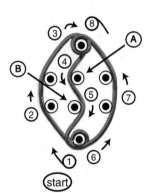

8 Pegs
5 Inches of 18 Gauge Wire

Tips: Form a loop down the wire. Place the loop on the starting peg, and follow the arrows to form the design.

To add a bead to the design, wrap through Arrow 4, bending the wire around peg A. Remove peg A and thread the bead onto the wire. Bend the wire around peg B, and complete the design.

Reduced in Size

Note: Pegs placed inside the wire design(s) on this page have been slightly adjusted for illustrative purposes. Please copy the peg placements on the jig template when making the design(s).

WigJig Olympus Template

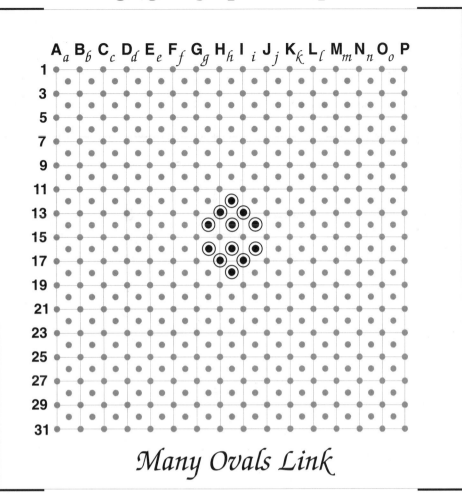

Many Ovals Link

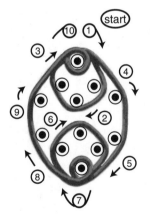

Enlarged to Show Detail

12 Pegs
7 Inches of 18 Gauge Wire

Tips: Form a loop down the wire. Place the loop on the starting peg, and follow the arrows to form the design. When bending the wire to form the inner circles, keep fingers close to the pegs. When making the large outer circle, hold fingers away from the pegs to form a smooth line. Flatten the wire with a metal dowel or other similar tool before removing the design from the jig.

Reduced in Size

© 1998, Helwig Industries, LLC
& Karen Ray

WigJig Olympus Template

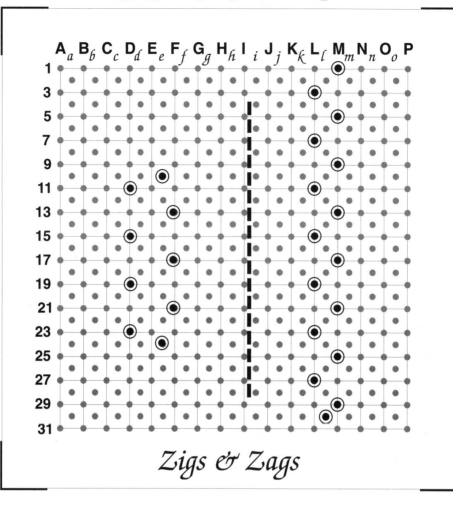

Zigs & Zags

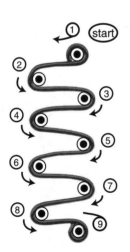

9 Pegs
8-1/2 Inches of 16 Gauge Wire

16 Pegs
10 Inches of 16 Gauge Wire

Tips: Form a loop up the wire. Place the loop on the starting peg, and follow the arrows to form the design. Remove the piece from the jig. Press the curves together with fingers or pliers to form desired shape.

Reduced in Size

WigJig Olympus Template

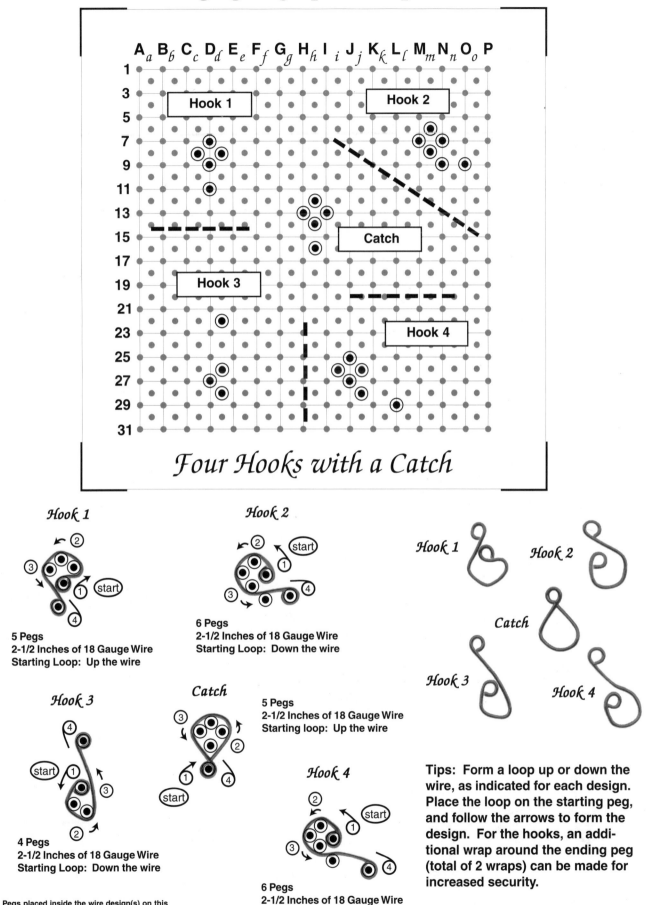

A_a B_b C_c D_d E_e F_f G_g H_h I_i J_j K_k L_l M_m N_n O_o P

Hook 1

Hook 2

Catch

Hook 3

Hook 4

Four Hooks with a Catch

Hook 1
5 Pegs
2-1/2 Inches of 18 Gauge Wire
Starting Loop: Up the wire

Hook 2
6 Pegs
2-1/2 Inches of 18 Gauge Wire
Starting Loop: Down the wire

Hook 3
4 Pegs
2-1/2 Inches of 18 Gauge Wire
Starting Loop: Down the wire

Catch
5 Pegs
2-1/2 Inches of 18 Gauge Wire
Starting loop: Up the wire

Hook 4
6 Pegs
2-1/2 Inches of 18 Gauge Wire
Starting Loop: Down the wire

Tips: Form a loop up or down the wire, as indicated for each design. Place the loop on the starting peg, and follow the arrows to form the design. For the hooks, an additional wrap around the ending peg (total of 2 wraps) can be made for increased security.

Note: Pegs placed inside the wire design(s) on this page have been slightly adjusted for illustrative purposes. Please copy the peg placements on the jig template when making the design(s).

WigJig Olympus Template

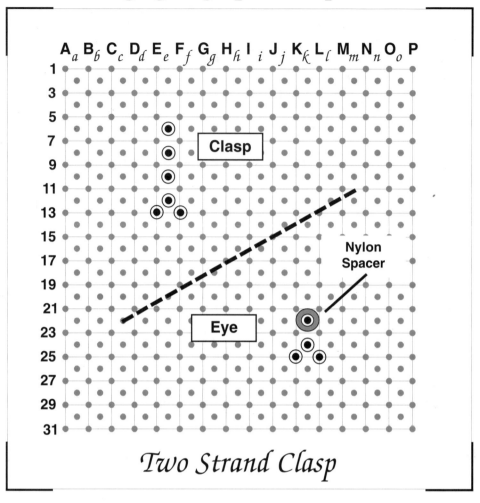

A_a B_b C_c D_d E_e F_f G_g H_h I_i J_j K_k L_l M_m N_n O_o P

1 3 5 7 9 11 13 15 17 19 21 23 25 27 29 31

Clasp

Eye

Nylon
Spacer

Two Strand Clasp

Clasp

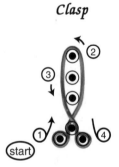

3
2
1   4
start

6 Pegs
4 Inches of 18 Gauge Wire

Tips: Form a loop up the wire. Place the
loop on the starting peg, and follow the
arrows to form the design. Remove the clasp
from the jig. Grip the clasp 1/2 inch from the
end using round nose pliers *(Figure 1)*. Bend
the end of the clasp around the nose of the
pliers to form the hook *(Figure 2)*.

Figure 1

Grip clasp between nose
of pliers here

Figure 2

Eye

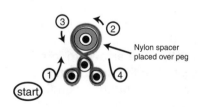

3
2
1   4
start

Nylon spacer
placed over peg

4 Pegs
1 Nylon Spacer (1/4 inch diameter)
5 Inches of 18 Gauge Wire

Tips: Place the nylon spacer on the
top peg. Form a loop up the wire.
Place the loop on the starting peg,
and follow the arrows to form the
design.

Note: Pegs placed inside the wire design(s) on this
page have been slightly adjusted for illustrative
purposes. Please copy the peg placements on the jig
template when making the design(s).

WigJig Olympus Template

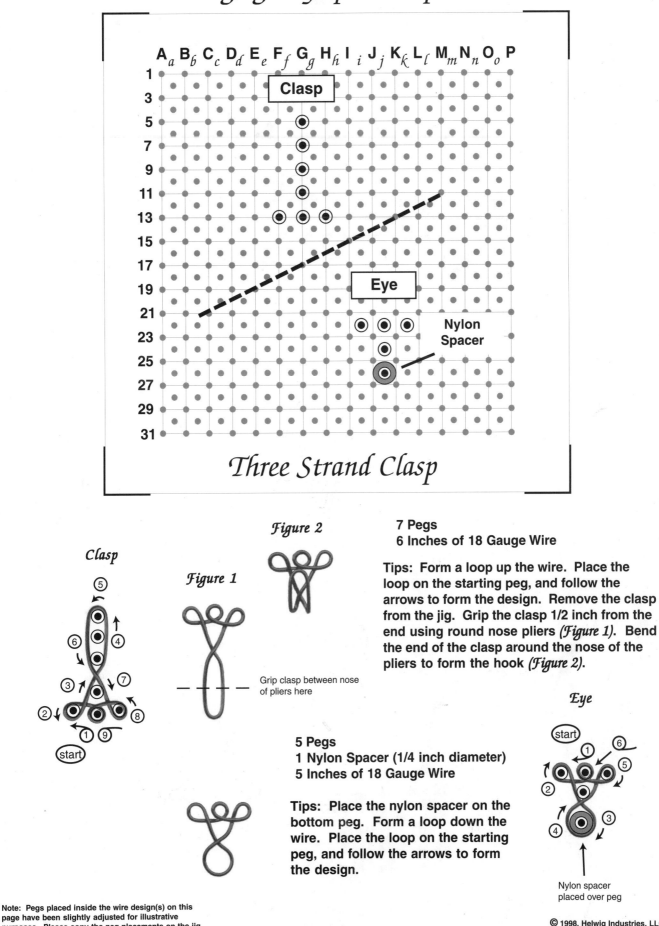

Clasp

Eye

Nylon Spacer

Three Strand Clasp

Clasp

Figure 1

Figure 2

Grip clasp between nose of pliers here

7 Pegs
6 Inches of 18 Gauge Wire

Tips: Form a loop up the wire. Place the loop on the starting peg, and follow the arrows to form the design. Remove the clasp from the jig. Grip the clasp 1/2 inch from the end using round nose pliers *(Figure 1)*. Bend the end of the clasp around the nose of the pliers to form the hook *(Figure 2)*.

Eye

start

5 Pegs
1 Nylon Spacer (1/4 inch diameter)
5 Inches of 18 Gauge Wire

Tips: Place the nylon spacer on the bottom peg. Form a loop down the wire. Place the loop on the starting peg, and follow the arrows to form the design.

Nylon spacer placed over peg

Note: Pegs placed inside the wire design(s) on this page have been slightly adjusted for illustrative purposes. Please copy the peg placements on the jig template when making the design(s).

(Page intentionally left blank)

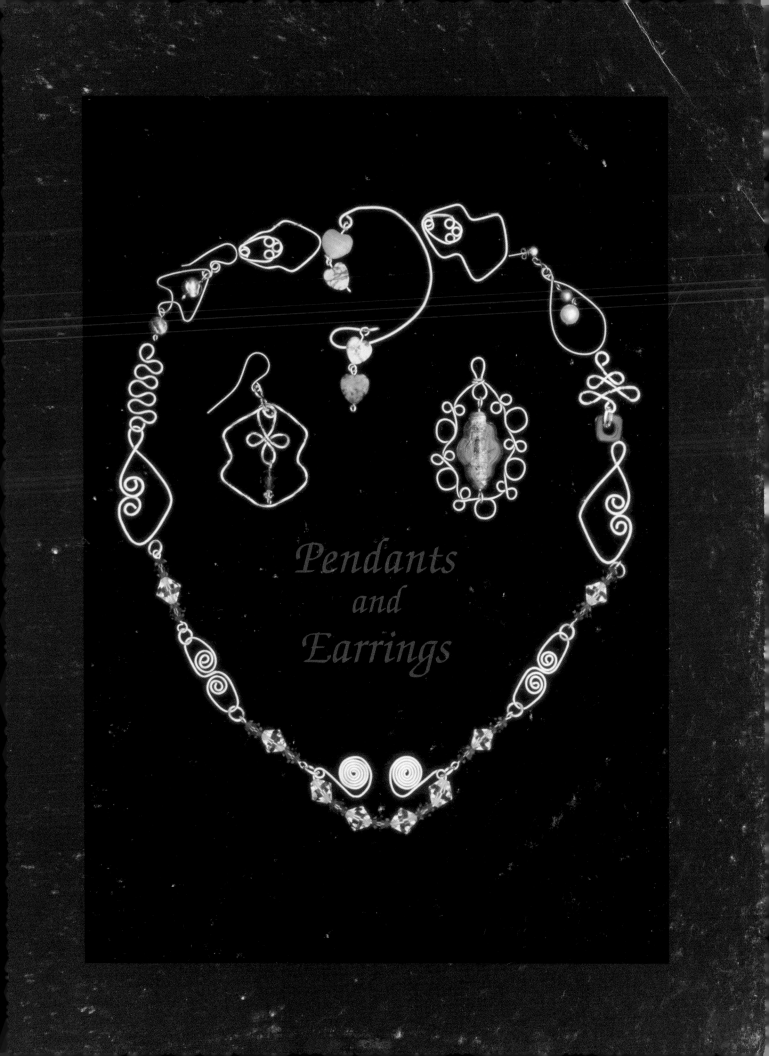

Pendants
and
Earrings

Wire designs in photograph on reverse side: Double Swirls (pg. 12), Rock & Roll (pg. 13), Helwig Classic (pg. 23), Zigs & Zags (pg. 42), Marj's Ear Cuff (pgs. 68 and 69), Petite Pendants (pgs. 71 and 72), Versatility (pg. 73), Eights & O's (pg 80), Lasso Frame Drops (pg. 90), and Swing & Swirl (pg. 91)

WigJig Olympus Template

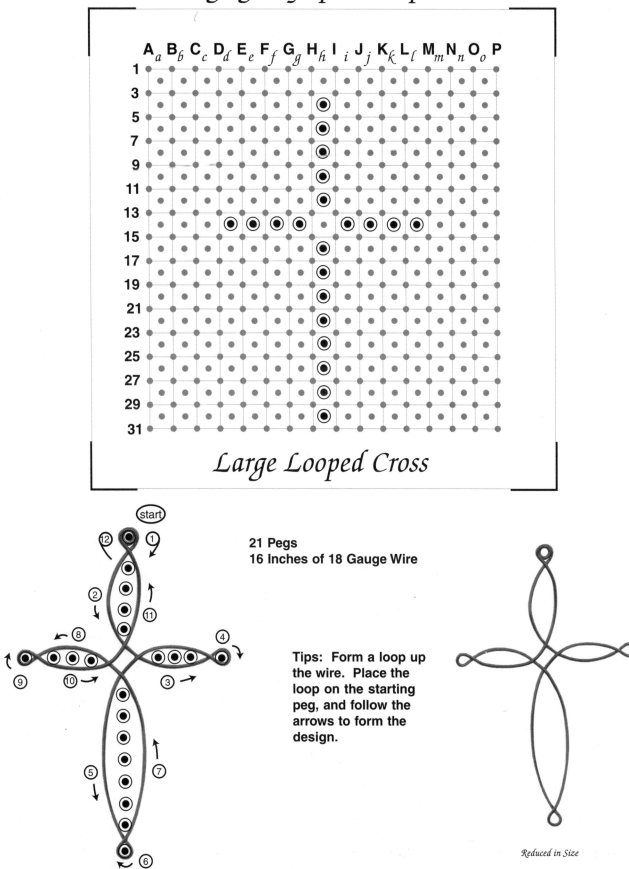

A_a B_b C_c D_d E_e F_f G_g H_h I_i J_j K_k L_l M_m N_n O_o P

Large Looped Cross

start

21 Pegs
16 Inches of 18 Gauge Wire

Tips: Form a loop up the wire. Place the loop on the starting peg, and follow the arrows to form the design.

Reduced in Size

Note: Pegs placed inside the wire design(s) on this page have been slightly adjusted for illustrative purposes. Please copy the peg placements on the jig template when making the design(s).

WigJig Olympus Template

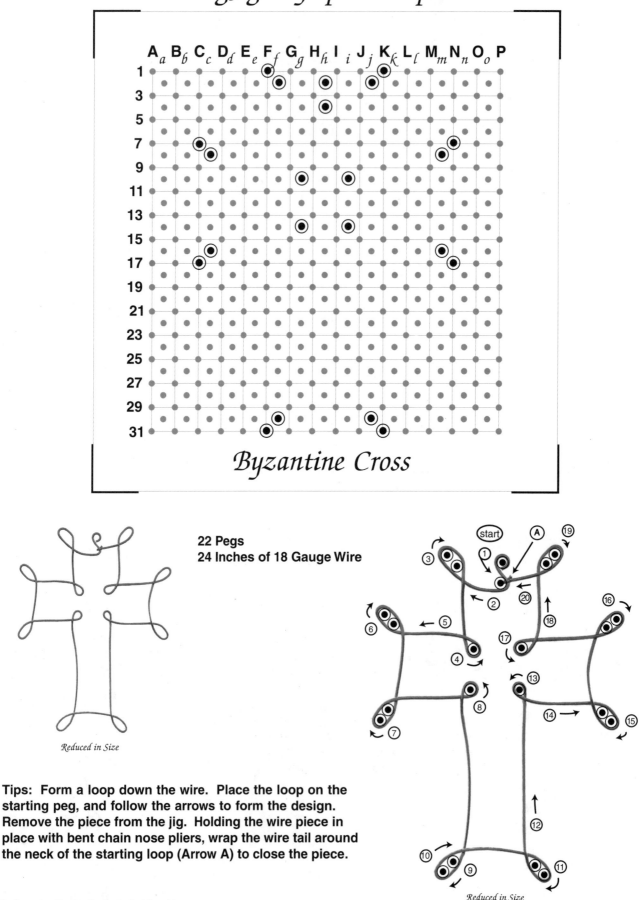

Byzantine Cross

22 Pegs
24 Inches of 18 Gauge Wire

Tips: Form a loop down the wire. Place the loop on the starting peg, and follow the arrows to form the design. Remove the piece from the jig. Holding the wire piece in place with bent chain nose pliers, wrap the wire tail around the neck of the starting loop (Arrow A) to close the piece.

Reduced in Size

WigJig Olympus Template

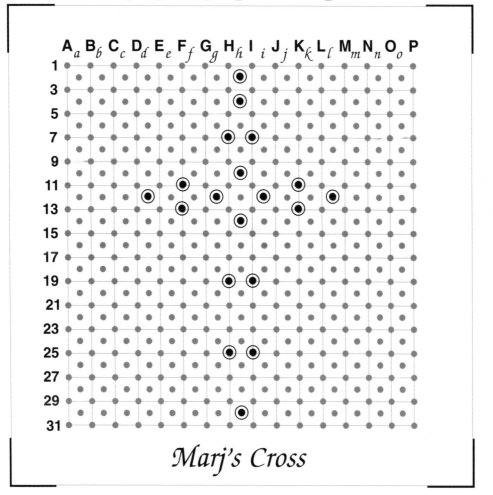

Marj's Cross

19 Pegs
13 Inches of 18 Gauge Wire

Tips: Form an eye loop, and place it on the starting peg. Follow the arrows to form the design. At Arrow A, bend the wire sharply around the final peg. Remove the design from the jig.

Holding the wire piece in place with bent chain nose pliers, wrap the wire tail around the neck of the starting loop (Arrow A) to close the piece.

Reduced in Size

For tips in forming an eye loop, see *"How to Make an Eye Loop"* in the *"Wire Working Tips & Hints"* chapter.

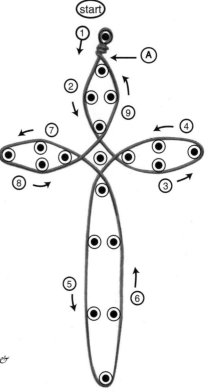

WigJig Olympus Template

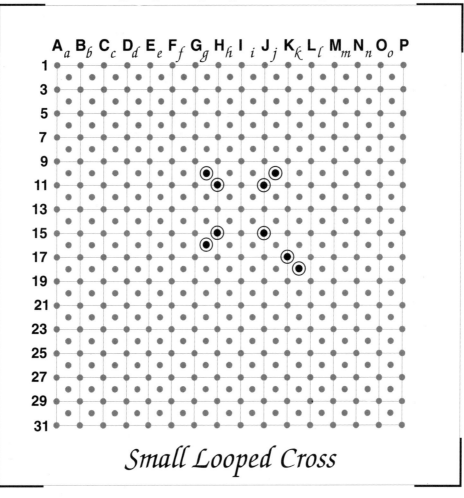

A a B b C c D d E e F f G g H h I i J j K k L l M m N n O o P

1 3 5 7 9 11 13 15 17 19 21 23 25 27 29 31

Small Looped Cross

9 Pegs
10 Inches of 18 Gauge Wire

Tips: Form a loop down the wire. Place the loop on the starting peg, and follow the arrows to form the design.

WigJig Olympus Template

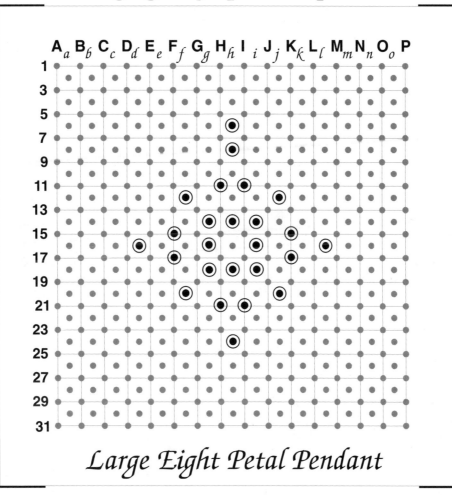

A _a_ B _b_ C _c_ D _d_ E _e_ F _f_ G _g_ H _h_ I _i_ J _j_ K _k_ L _l_ M _m_ N _n_ O _o_ P

1 3 5 7 9 11 13 15 17 19 21 23 25 27 29 31

Large Eight Petal Pendant

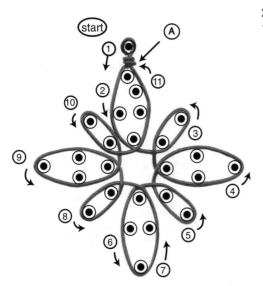

start
A
1
11
2
10
3
9
4
8
5
6
7

25 Pegs
16 Inches of 18 Gauge Wire

Tips: Form an eye loop in the wire. Place the loop on the starting peg, and follow the arrows to form the design. Remove from the jig.

Holding the design with bent chain nose pliers, wrap the wire tail around the neck of the starting loop (Arrow A), to anchor and complete the design.

To make an eye loop, please review the section _"How to Make an Eye Loop"_ in the _"Wire Working Tips & Hints"_ chapter.

Note: Pegs placed inside the wire design(s) on this page have been slightly adjusted for illustrative purposes. Please copy the peg placements on the jig template when making the design(s).

© 1998, Helwig Industries, LLC
& Karen Ray

53

Eight Petal Flower Pendants

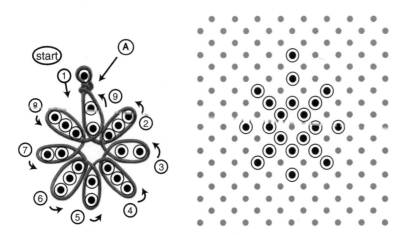

21 Pegs
14 Inches of 18 Gauge Wire (Basic)
17 Inches of 18 Gauge Wire (Filigree)
16 Inches of 20 Gauge Wire (Filigree)

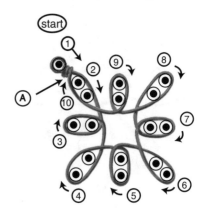

Tips: For these designs, form an eye loop in the wire. Place the loop on the starting peg, and follow the arrows to form the design. Remove from the jig.

Holding the wire piece with bent chain nose pliers, wrap the wire tail around the neck of the starting loop (Arrow A) to anchor and complete the design.

Filigree Variation

Variation: The filigree variation to the left is made by omitting the starting peg (Arrow 1), and wrapping completely around the outermost peg for each petal, using 18 or 20 gauge wire.

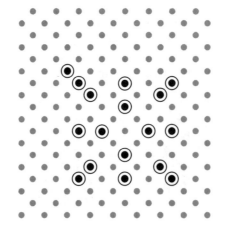

17 Pegs
14 Inches of 18 Gauge Wire

To make an eye loop, please review the section *"How to Make an Eye Loop"* in the *"Wire Working Tips & Hints"* chapter.

Note: Pegs placed inside the wire design(s) on this page have been slightly adjusted for illustrative purposes. Please copy the peg placements on the jig template when making the design(s).

WigJig Olympus Template

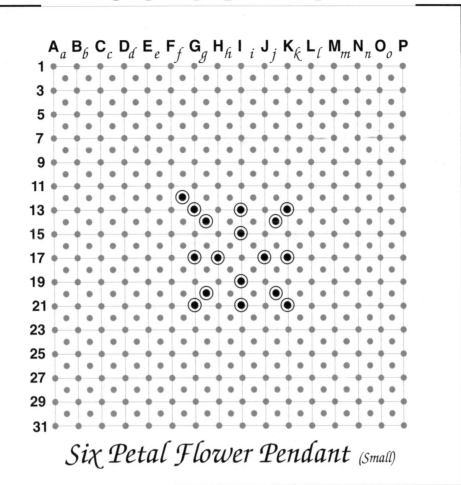

A_a B_b C_c D_d E_e F_f G_g H_h I_i J_j K_k L_l M_m N_n O_o P

1 3 5 7 9 11 13 15 17 19 21 23 25 27 29 31

Six Petal Flower Pendant (Small)

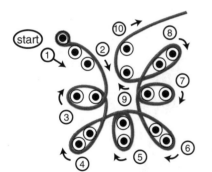

Reduced in Size

17 Pegs
12 Inches of 18 Gauge Wire

Tips: Form an eye loop in the wire. Place the loop on the starting peg, and follow the arrows to form the design. Remove the design from the jig.

Using chain nose pliers, bend the wire tail 90 degrees upward and forward at Arrow A. In other words, with the piece facing you, the wire tail will be pointing toward you. Wrap the wire tail around the center of the flower at Arrow B twice. Line up the final loop (Arrow D) with the first petal (Arrow C).

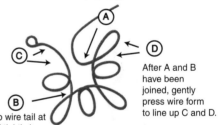

Bend wire tail 90 degrees up and towards you.

After A and B have been joined, gently press wire form to line up C and D.

Wrap wire tail at bend tightly here.

Reduced in Size

Variation (not shown): A filigree variation can be made by wrapping completely around the outermost peg for each petal.

To make an eye loop, please review the section *"How to Make an Eye Loop"* in the *"Wire Working Tips & Hints"* chapter.

Note: Pegs placed inside the wire design(s) on this page have been slightly adjusted for illustrative purposes. Please copy the peg placements on the jig template when making the design(s).

WigJig Olympus Template

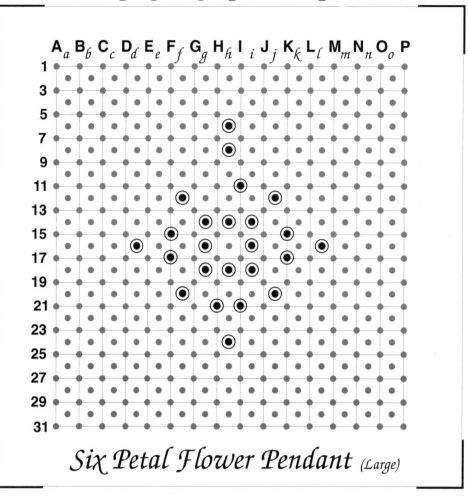

A_a B_b C_c D_d E_e F_f G_g H_h I_i J_j K_k L_l M_m N_n O_o P

1 3 5 7 9 11 13 15 17 19 21 23 25 27 29 31

Six Petal Flower Pendant *(Large)*

24 Pegs
14 Inches of 18 Gauge Wire

This piece is wrapped identically to the *"Six Petal Flower Pendant (Small)"*. Please see prior page for detailed instructions.

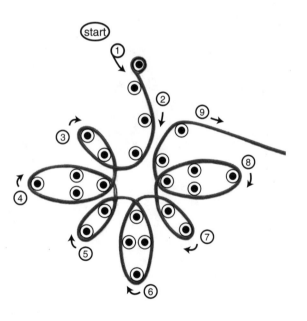

Note: Pegs placed inside the wire design(s) on this page have been slightly adjusted for illustrative purposes. Please copy the peg placements on the jig template when making the design(s).

WigJig Olympus Template

A_a B_b C_c D_d E_e F_f G_g H_h I_i J_j K_k L_l M_m N_n O_o P

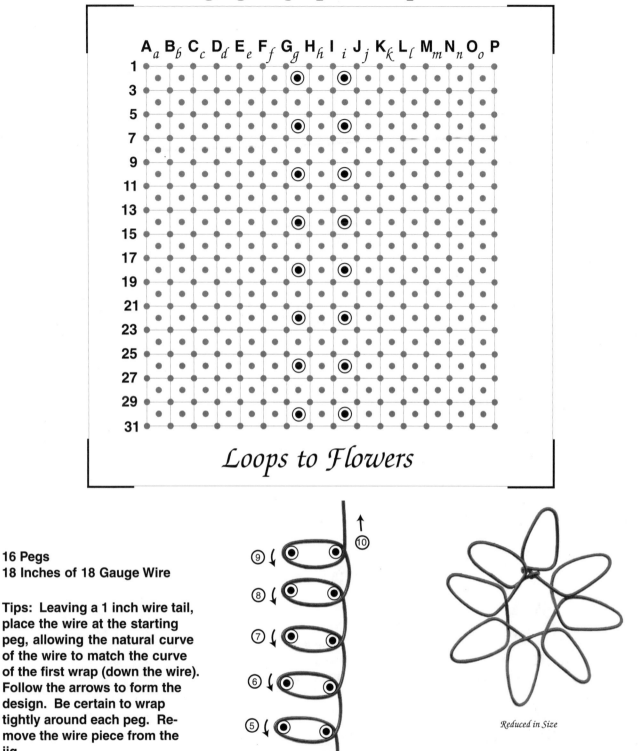

Loops to Flowers

16 Pegs
18 Inches of 18 Gauge Wire

Tips: Leaving a 1 inch wire tail, place the wire at the starting peg, allowing the natural curve of the wire to match the curve of the first wrap (down the wire). Follow the arrows to form the design. Be certain to wrap tightly around each peg. Remove the wire piece from the jig.

Form the flower by bending the wire in a circle, as shown. Finish by twisting the wire tails around each other to secure.

Reduced in Size

Note: A smaller version of this design, called *"Six Petals"* can be found in the *"Chains & Links"* chapter.

For tips on starting a design "down the wire" without a starting loop, see *"How to Start at the Center of the Wire"* in the *"Wire Working Tips & Hints"* chapter.

Note: Pegs placed inside the wire design(s) on this page have been slightly adjusted for illustrative purposes. Please copy the peg placements on the jig template when making the design(s).

WigJig Olympus Template

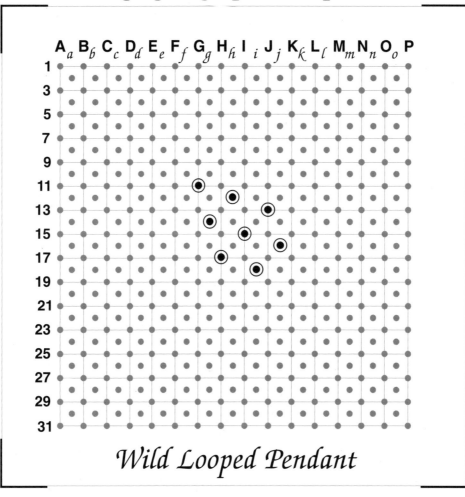

Wild Looped Pendant

8 Pegs
10 Inches of 18 Gauge Wire

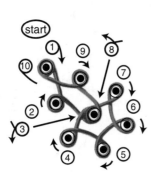

Tips: Form a loop down the wire. Place the loop on the starting peg, and follow the arrows to form the design.

Variation: Bend the top loop forward and the rear loop backward to form a three-dimensional piece. Attach beads to the loops.

Note: Pegs placed inside the wire design(s) on this page have been slightly adjusted for illustrative purposes. Please copy the peg placements on the jig template when making the design(s).

WigJig Olympus Template

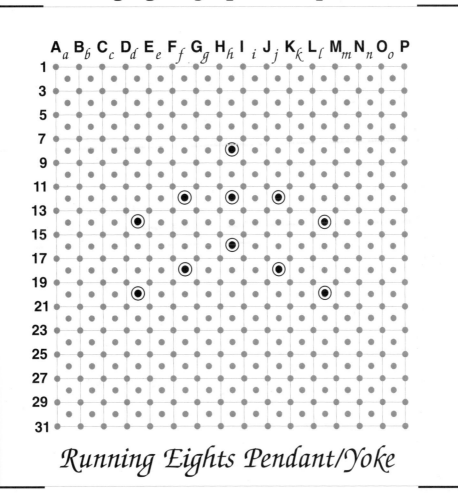

A $_a$ B $_b$ C $_c$ D $_d$ E $_e$ F $_f$ G $_g$ H $_h$ I $_i$ J $_j$ K $_k$ L $_l$ M $_m$ N $_n$ O $_o$ P

1
3
5
7
9
11
13
15
17
19
21
23
25
27
29
31

Running Eights Pendant/Yoke

11 Pegs
10 Inches of 18 Gauge Wire

Tips: Form a loop down the wire. Place the loop on the starting peg, and follow the arrows to form the design.

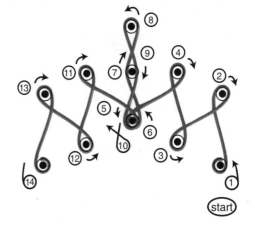

Reduced in Size

© 1998, Helwig Industries, LLC
& Karen Ray

WigJig Olympus Template

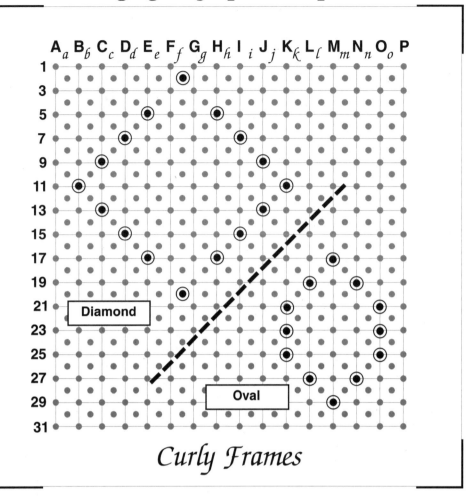

A_a B_b C_c D_d E_e F_f G_g H_h I_i J_j K_k L_l M_m N_n O_o P

Diamond

Oval

Curly Frames

Diamond

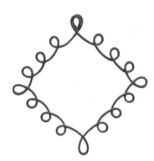

Reduced in Size

16 Pegs
15 Inches of 18 Gauge Wire

For tips on starting a design in the center of the wire, see *"How to Start at the Center of the Wire"* in the *"Wire Working Tips & Hints"* chapter.

Tips: Measure, then place the center of the wire below the starting peg, letting the natural curve of the wire follow the curve of the first wrap (down the wire). Wrap the first wire tail through Arrow 7. Holding this wire tail in place, return to the starting pegs at Arrow 8, and fully wrap the other wire tail to complete the design.

Oval

Remove from jig. Tuck ending loop behind starting loop to lock design into place.

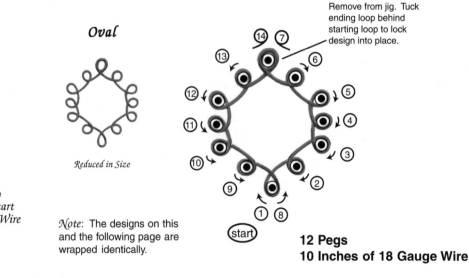

Reduced in Size

Note: The designs on this and the following page are wrapped identically.

12 Pegs
10 Inches of 18 Gauge Wire

12 Pegs
18 Inches of 18 Gauge Wire

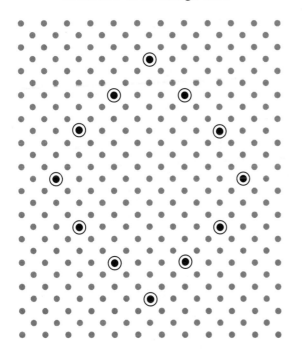

Large Curly Frame

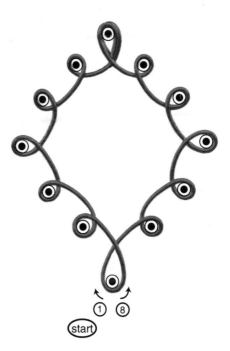

Instructions for making these pendants can be found on the previous page.

Victorian Pendant

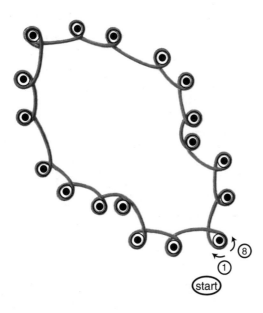

18 Pegs
18 Inches of 18 Gauge Wire

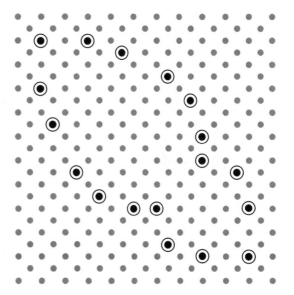

Note: Pegs placed inside the wire designs on this page have been slightly adjusted for illustrative purposes. Please copy the peg placements on the jig template when making this design.

WigJig Olympus Template

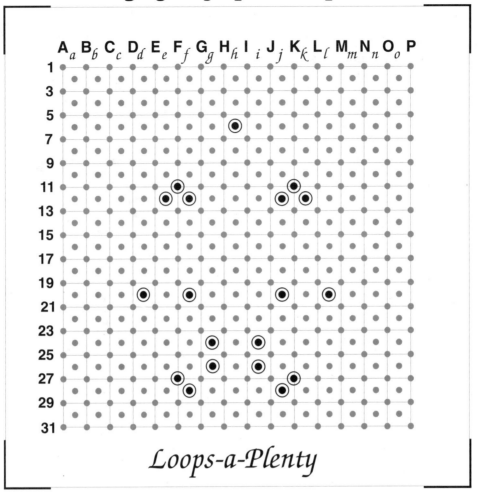

A a B b C c D d E e F f G g H h I i J j K k L l M m N n O o P

Loops-a-Plenty

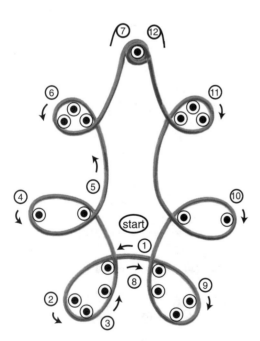

19 Pegs
18 Inches of 18 Gauge Wire
19 Inches of 16 Gauge Wire

Tips: Measure, then place the center of the wire over the top of the starting pegs (Arrow 1), letting the natural curve of the wire follow the curve of the first wrap (down the wire). Wrap the first wire tail to form one side of the pendant. Return to the starting pegs at Arrow 8, and follow the arrows to complete the design.

Reduced in Size

For tips on starting a design in the center of the wire, see *"How to Start at the Center of the Wire"* in the *"Wire Working Tips & Hints"* chapter.

WigJig Olympus Template

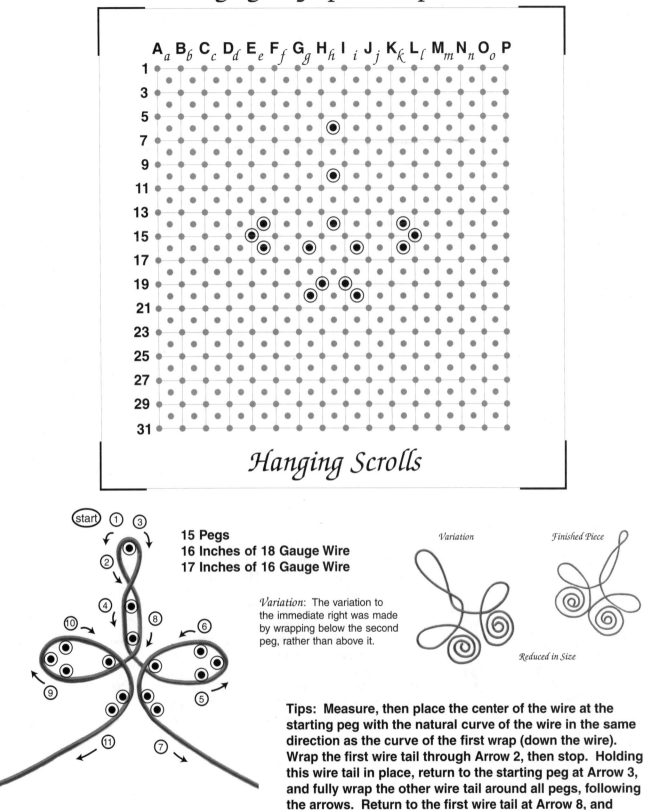

Hanging Scrolls

15 Pegs
16 Inches of 18 Gauge Wire
17 Inches of 16 Gauge Wire

Variation: The variation to the immediate right was made by wrapping below the second peg, rather than above it.

Variation

Finished Piece

Reduced in Size

Tips: Measure, then place the center of the wire at the starting peg with the natural curve of the wire in the same direction as the curve of the first wrap (down the wire). Wrap the first wire tail through Arrow 2, then stop. Holding this wire tail in place, return to the starting peg at Arrow 3, and fully wrap the other wire tail around all pegs, following the arrows. Return to the first wire tail at Arrow 8, and complete its wrap. Trim both wire tails to 3-1/2 inches in length, and form scrolls or coils at each end.

For tips on making scrolls and coils, see *"How to Make a Coil or Scroll"* in the *"Wire Working Tips & Hints"* chapter.

WigJig Olympus Template

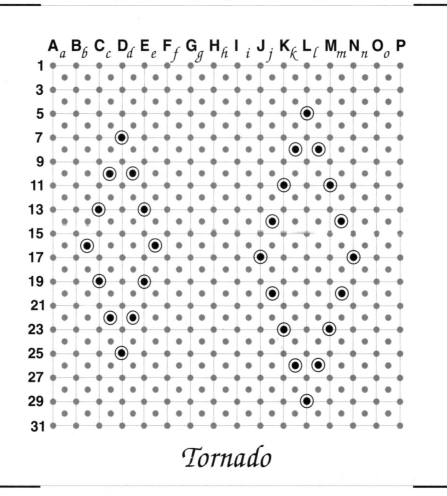

A_a B_b C_c D_d E_e F_f G_g H_h I_i J_j K_k L_l M_m N_n O_o P

Rows: 1, 3, 5, 7, 9, 11, 13, 15, 17, 19, 21, 23, 25, 27, 29, 31

Tornado

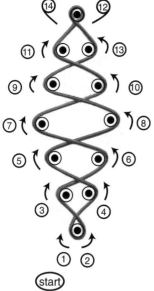

(14) (12)
(11) (13)
(9) (10)
(7) (8)
(5) (6)
(3) (4)
(1) (2)
(start)

Tips: Measure, then place the center of the wire at the starting peg with the natural curve of the wire in the same direction as the curve of the first wrap (down the wire). Wrap the first wire tail around the pegs through Arrow 2, then stop. Holding this wire tail in place, wrap the other wire tail around 2 more pegs, then stop. Switch back to the first wire tail at the starting peg and wrap around the next 2 pegs, and stop. Continue wrapping around 2 pegs for each wire tail, then changing to the other wire tail, until the piece is fully wrapped at the top. This wrapping technique is similar to braiding or lacing a shoe.

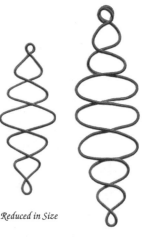

Reduced in Size

12 Pegs (small design)
16 Pegs (large design)
12 Inches of 18 Gauge Wire (small design)
18 Inches of 16 Gauge Wire (large design)

For tips on starting a design in the center of the wire, see *"How to Start at the Center of the Wire"* in the *"Wire Working Tips & Hints"* chapter.

WigJig Olympus Template

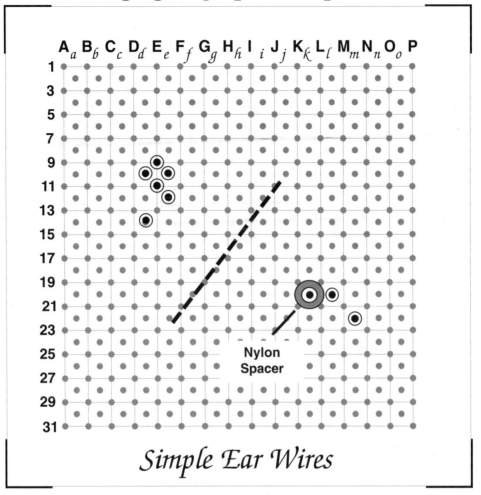

A_a B_b C_c D_d E_e F_f G_g H_h I_i J_j K_k L_l M_m N_n O_o P

Nylon Spacer

Simple Ear Wires

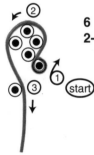

6 Pegs
2-1/2 Inches of 20 Gauge Wire

Tips: For both designs, form a loop up the wire. Place the loop on the starting peg, and follow the arrows to form the design. Remove from the jig, and file the end of the ear wire to smooth.

Note: We recommend using 20 or 22 gauge wire for ear wires. A smaller gauge (thicker wire) may not be comfortable, and larger gauge (finer wire) may tear the ear hole.

3 Pegs
1 Nylon Spacer (3/8 inch outer diameter)
2-1/2 Inches of 20 Gauge Wire

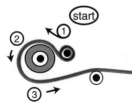

Note: You can make earring wires without the jig by cutting a 2-1/2 inch piece of wire and making a loop up the wire. Hook the loop under the cap of a ballpoint pen and bend the wire 7/8 of the way around the cap. The ear wires for the *"Diamond Maze"* and the *"Small Diamond Drop"* were made using this method. The extra bend in these ear wires helps keep them in place.

Variation (not shown): For a more secure piece, form the starting loop 1 inch from the end of the wire, leaving a wire tail. Form the design, remove from the jig and wrap the 1 inch wire tail around the neck of the starting loop. Clip ends.

Note: Pegs placed inside the wire design(s) on this page have been slightly adjusted for illustrative purposes. Please copy the peg placements on the jig template when making the design(s).

Tiny Single-Wrap Earrings

Four Petal Flower, Trefoil, Cross, and Wrapped Figure 8: **Follow the arrows to form the design. Remove the piece from the jig, and harden the wire (flatten with fingers or nylon jaw pliers, or hammer lightly). Turn the piece over with the back facing you and with the wire tail on top. Bend the wire tail 90 degrees forward from the plane of the piece. In other words, if the back of the piece is facing you, the wire tail will be pointing toward you, as shown in *Figure 1*. This will form the post for the earring. Harden the design again by gently pressing between the jaws of nylon pliers or hammering lightly. Trim the earring post to 1/2 inch in length, and file the end to round and smooth. Use purchased earring backs (found in jewelry stores) to hold the earring in place.**

Figure 1

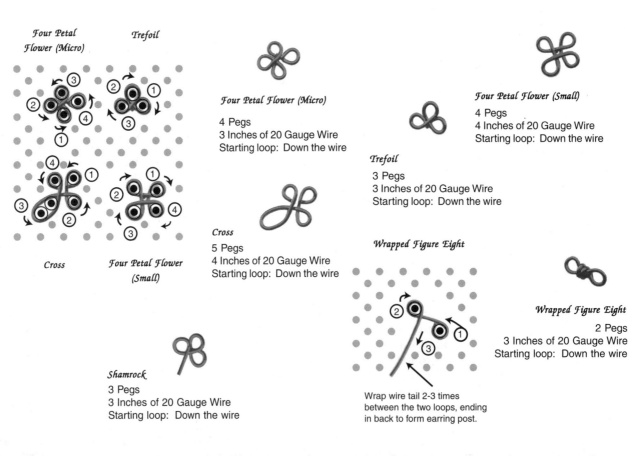

Four Petal Flower (Micro)

Trefoil

Four Petal Flower (Micro)

4 Pegs
3 Inches of 20 Gauge Wire
Starting loop: Down the wire

Four Petal Flower (Small)

4 Pegs
4 Inches of 20 Gauge Wire
Starting loop: Down the wire

Trefoil

3 Pegs
3 Inches of 20 Gauge Wire
Starting loop: Down the wire

Cross

5 Pegs
4 Inches of 20 Gauge Wire
Starting loop: Down the wire

Cross

Four Petal Flower (Small)

Wrapped Figure Eight

Wrapped Figure Eight

2 Pegs
3 Inches of 20 Gauge Wire
Starting loop: Down the wire

Wrap wire tail 2-3 times between the two loops, ending in back to form earring post.

Shamrock

3 Pegs
3 Inches of 20 Gauge Wire
Starting loop: Down the wire

Shamrock: **This is a variation of the *Three Petal Flower* shown above. Make a loop 1/2 inch from the end of the wire (down the wire). The 1/2 inch wire tail will form the "stem" of the shamrock. Form the design as shown for the *Three Petal Flower*. Remove the piece from the jig, being certain to harden the wire (flatten with fingers or nylon jaw pliers, or hammer lightly). Turn the piece over with the back facing you and with the second wire tail on top. Bend the wire tail 90 degrees forward from the plane of the piece. In other words, if the back of the piece is facing you, the second wire tail will be pointing toward you, as shown in *Figure 1*. This second wire tail becomes the post for the earring. Trim the earring post to 1/2 inch in length, and file the end to round and smooth. Use purchased earring backs (found in jewelry stores) to hold the earring in place.**

Note: Pegs placed inside the wire design(s) on this page have been slightly adjusted for illustrative purposes. Please copy the peg placements on the jig template when making the design(s).

Tiny Single-Wrap Earrings (continued)

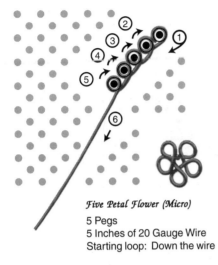

Five Petal Flower (Micro)
5 Pegs
5 Inches of 20 Gauge Wire
Starting loop: Down the wire

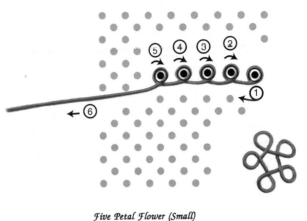

Five Petal Flower (Small)
5 Pegs
5 Inches of 20 Gauge Wire
Starting loop: Down the wire

Five Petal Flowers: **Wrap the wire as indicated by the arrows above. Remove the piece from the jig. Form the flower by bending the wire in a circle, as shown in the finished piece. Harden the wire by flattening with fingers or nylon jaw pliers, or hammer lightly. Turn the piece over with the back facing you and the wire tail on top. Bend the wire tail 90 degrees forward from the plane of the piece. In other words, if the back of the piece is facing you, the wire tail will be pointing toward you, as shown in *Figure 1*. This will form the post for the earring. Trim the earring post to 1/2 inch, and file the end to smooth and round. Use purchased earring backs (can be found in jewelry stores) to hold the earring in place.**

Figure 1

Scroll with Drop

4 Inches of 20
Gauge Wire

Coil
4 Inches of 20
Gauge Wire

Coil with Drop

4 Inches of 20
Gauge Wire

Scroll with Drop, Coil and Coil with Drop: **Approximately 1/2 inch from one end, place a 90 degree bend in the wire, using chain nose pliers, as shown in Figure 2. The short end of the wire will become the earring post.**

At the corner of the bend, form a tiny loop as shown in Figures 3 and 4. This tiny loop becomes the center of the coil/scroll. Grasp tiny loop in jaws of pliers and form the coil/scrolls. Trim earring post to 1/2 inch in length, and file to smooth and round.

A drop can be added after making the coil/scroll by forming a loop in the opposite direction from the coil/scroll. Be certain that the coils/scrolls/drops for these earrings are mirror images of each other.

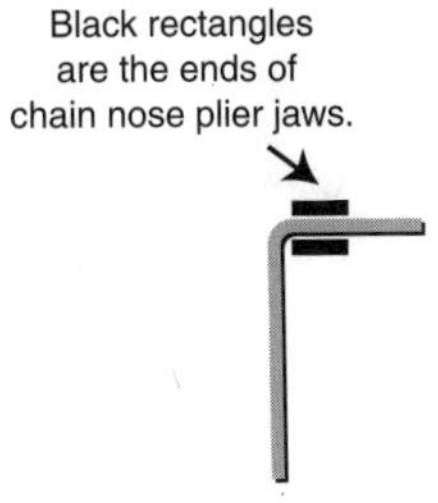

Black rectangles
are the ends of
chain nose plier jaws.

Figure 2

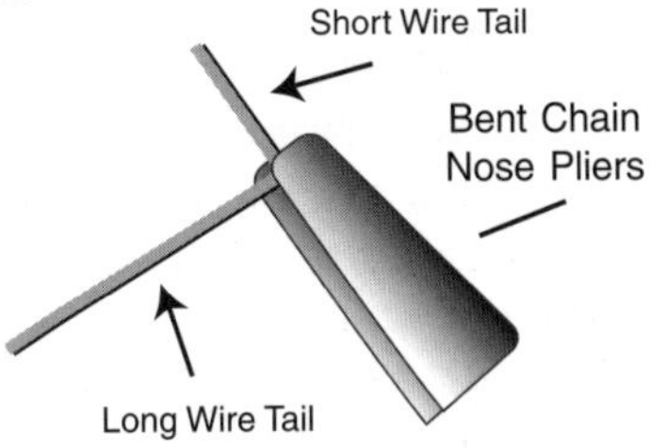

Short Wire Tail

Bent Chain
Nose Pliers

Long Wire Tail

Figure 3

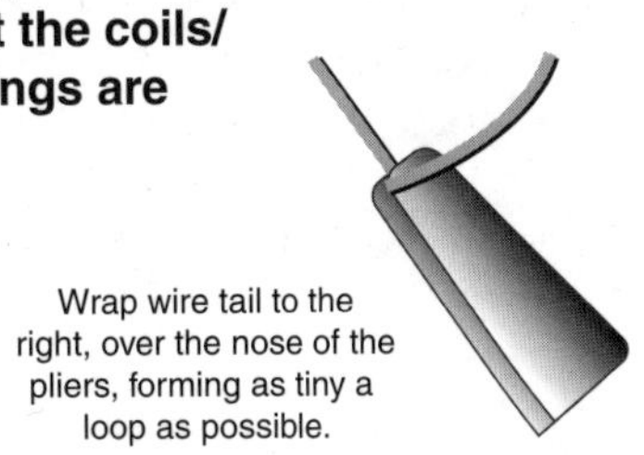

Wrap wire tail to the
right, over the nose of the
pliers, forming as tiny a
loop as possible.

Figure 4

Note: Wire lengths are estimated, since length depends on size of coils/scrolls desired.

WigJig Olympus Template

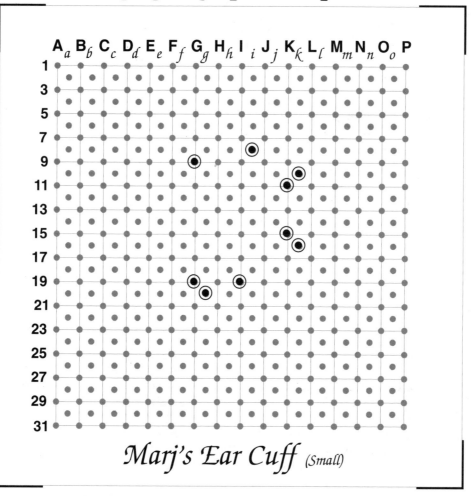

A a B b C c D d E e F f G g H h I i J j K k L l M m N n O o P

1
3
5
7
9
11
13
15
17
19
21
23
25
27
29
31

Marj's Ear Cuff (Small)

9 Pegs
6 Inches of 16 Gauge Wire

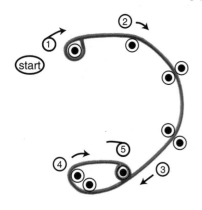

Tips: Form a loop down the wire. Place the loop on the starting peg, and follow the arrows to form the design. Remove the cuff from the jig. Place the wire piece on a flat surface in the orientation shown in *Figure 1*. At arrow A, bend the wire inside the ellipse forward. In other words, the wire will be bent outward and towards you. This final bend allows beads on the ending loop to hang freely, and helps secure the cuff on the ear.

Place the remaining earring cuff in the "mirror image" orientation shown in *Figure 2*. Finish as outlined above.

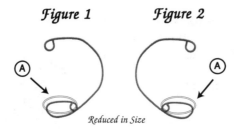

Figure 1   *Figure 2*

Reduced in Size

Note: Sections of the wire piece to be bent forward in step 2 are enclosed in the ellipses.

Reduced in Size

WigJig Olympus Template

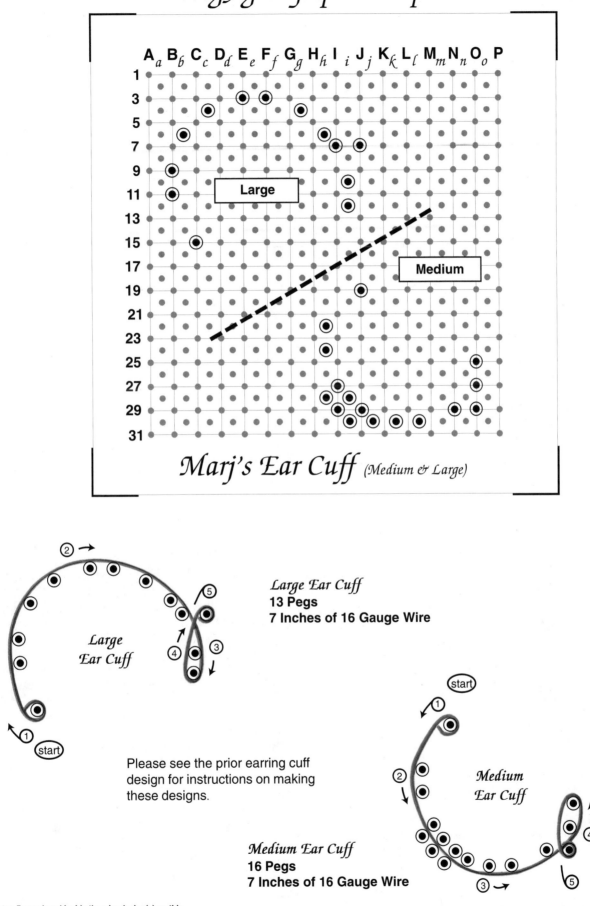

A B C D E F G H I J K L M N O P
1 3 5 7 9 11 13 15 17 19 21 23 25 27 29 31

Large

Medium

Marj's Ear Cuff (Medium & Large)

Large Ear Cuff
13 Pegs
7 Inches of 16 Gauge Wire

Large Ear Cuff

Please see the prior earring cuff design for instructions on making these designs.

Medium Ear Cuff
16 Pegs
7 Inches of 16 Gauge Wire

start

Medium Ear Cuff

Note: Pegs placed inside the wire design(s) on this page have been slightly adjusted for illustrative purposes. Please copy the peg placements on the jig template when making the design(s).

© 1998, Helwig Industries, LLC

69

WigJig Olympus Template

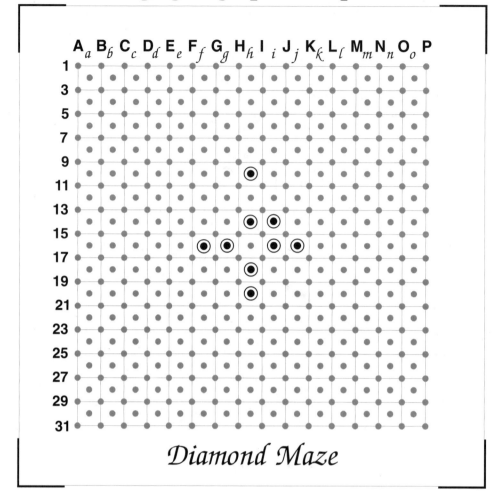

Diamond Maze

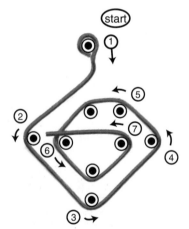

start

9 Pegs
6 Inches of 18 Gauge Wire

For tips in forming an eye loop, see *"How to Make an Eye Loop"* in the *"Wire Working Tips & Hints"* chapter.

Place round nose pliers here.

Ⓐ

Ⓑ

45 degree angle formed around nose of pliers.

Figure 1

Tips: Form an eye loop in one end of the wire. Place round nose pliers approximately 1/8 inch below the loop (*Figure 1*, Arrow A). Bend the wire 45 degrees around the nose of the pliers to form an angle in the wire (*Figure 1*, Arrow B). Place the wire on the starting peg, and follow the arrows to form the design. Hold fingers close to the pegs when wrapping in order to achieve the sharp angles integral to this design. Press wire gently with a dowel or other similar tool, and remove the piece from the jig. Thread a bead onto the wire, and form a tiny loop at the end to complete the design.

Reduced in Size

Note: Pegs placed inside the wire design(s) on this page have been slightly adjusted for illustrative purposes. Please copy the peg placements on the jig template when making the design(s).

WigJig Olympus Template

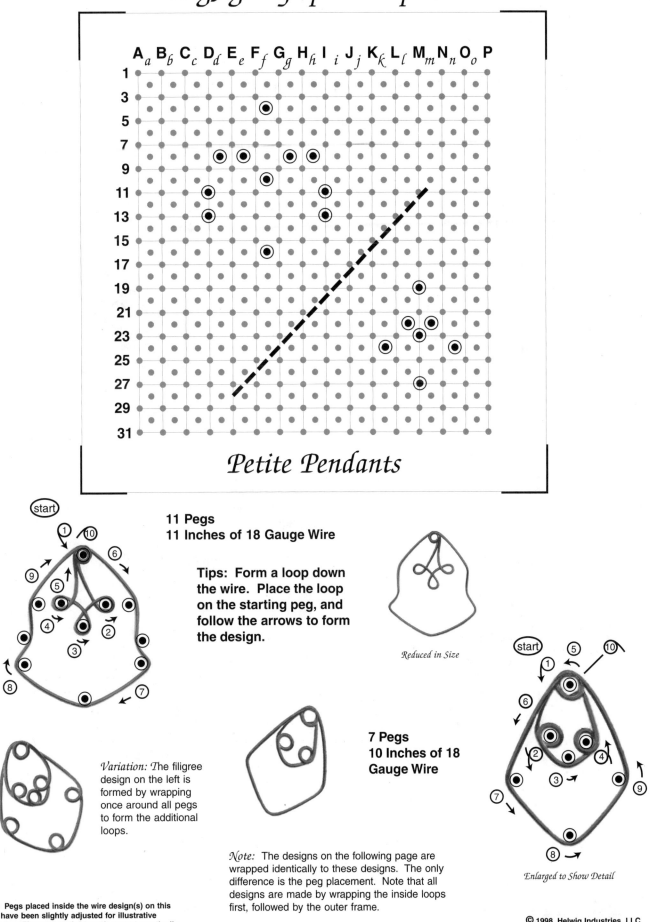

Petite Pendants

11 Pegs
11 Inches of 18 Gauge Wire

Tips: Form a loop down the wire. Place the loop on the starting peg, and follow the arrows to form the design.

Reduced in Size

Variation: The filigree design on the left is formed by wrapping once around all pegs to form the additional loops.

7 Pegs
10 Inches of 18 Gauge Wire

Note: The designs on the following page are wrapped identically to these designs. The only difference is the peg placement. Note that all designs are made by wrapping the inside loops first, followed by the outer frame.

Enlarged to Show Detail

Note: Pegs placed inside the wire design(s) on this page have been slightly adjusted for illustrative purposes. Please copy the peg placements on the jig template when making the design(s).

Petite Pendants *(Continued)*

(Directions can be found on the prior page)

7 Pegs
10 Inches of 18 Gauge Wire

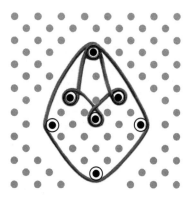

9 Pegs
10 Inches of 18 Gauge Wire

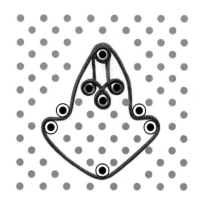

Instructions for making these designs can be found on the previous page.

7 Pegs
10 Inches of 18 Gauge Wire

9 Pegs
9 Inches of 18 Gauge Wire

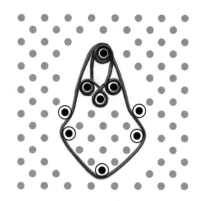

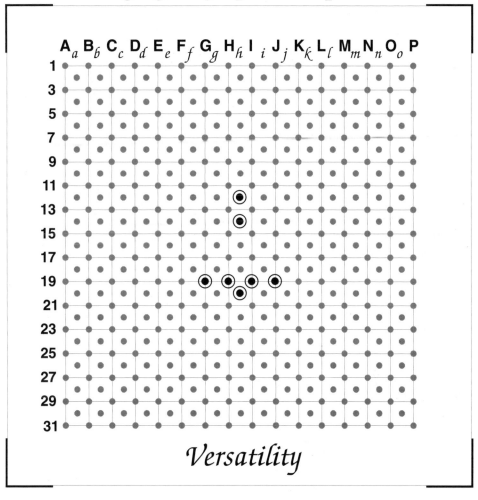

A $_a$ B $_b$ C $_c$ D $_d$ E $_e$ F $_f$ G $_g$ H $_h$ I $_i$ J $_j$ K $_k$ L $_l$ M $_m$ N $_n$ O $_o$ P

Versatility

7 Pegs
9 Inches of 18 Gauge Wire

Tips: Form a loop down the wire. Place the loop on the starting peg, and follow the arrows to form the design. Keep fingers close to the pegs while bending the wire. Flatten the wire with a metal dowel or other similar tool before removing the design from the jig.

Reduced in Size

Variations: These designs are all formed using the same peg pattern. They differ in the loops that are wrapped and the direction of the wrap. All designs require approximately 7 inches of 18 or 20 gauge wire.

Note: Pegs placed inside the wire design(s) on this page have been slightly adjusted for illustrative purposes. Please copy the peg placements on the jig template when making the design(s).

WigJig Olympus Template

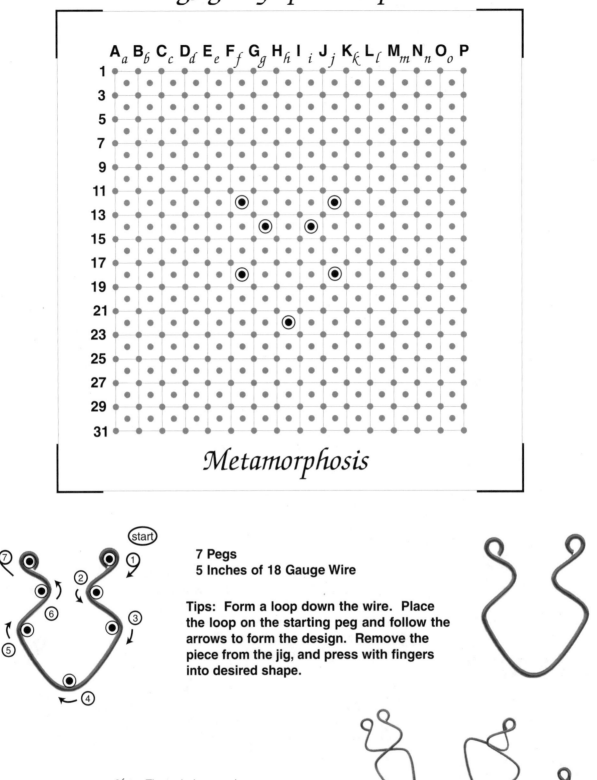

Metamorphosis

7 Pegs
5 Inches of 18 Gauge Wire

Tips: Form a loop down the wire. Place the loop on the starting peg and follow the arrows to form the design. Remove the piece from the jig, and press with fingers into desired shape.

start ①②③④⑤⑥⑦

Note: These designs can be used as pendants, links, purse handles, or with art glass.

Reduced in Size

Note: Pegs placed inside the wire design(s) on this page have been slightly adjusted for illustrative purposes. Please copy the peg placements on the jig template when making the design(s).

WigJig Olympus Template

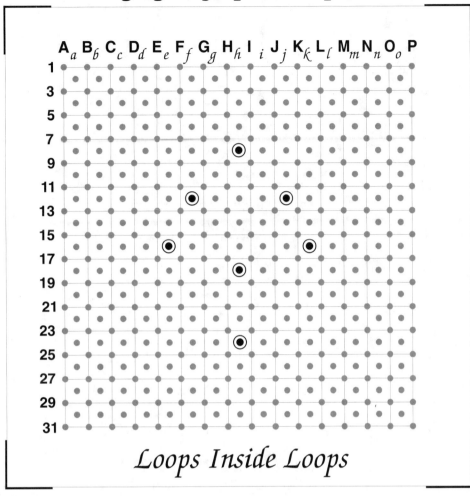

A a B b C c D d E e F f G g H h I i J j K k L l M m N n O o P

1 3 5 7 9 11 13 15 17 19 21 23 25 27 29 31

Loops Inside Loops

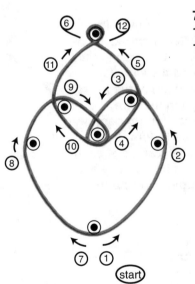

7 Pegs
13 Inches of 18 Gauge Wire
14 Inches of 16 Gauge Wire

Tips: Place the center of the wire below the bottom peg, letting the natural curve of the wire follow the curve of the first wrap (down the wire). Wrap the first wire tail, following the arrows, as shown. Return to the starting peg, and fully wrap the other wire tail to finish the piece.

Reduced in Size

For tips on starting a design in the center of the wire, see *"How to Start at the Center of the Wire"* in the *"Wire Working Tips & Hints"* chapter.

WigJig Olympus Template

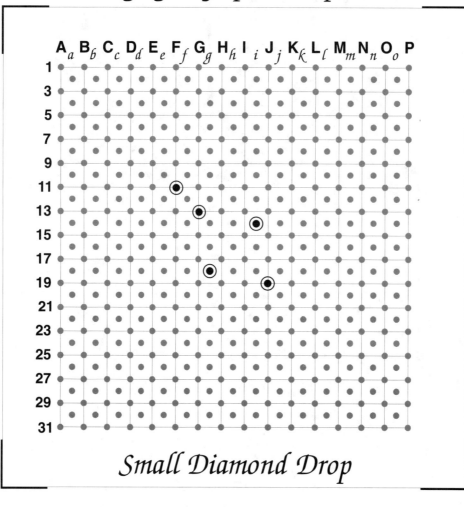

A_a B_b C_c D_d E_e F_f G_g H_h I_i J_j K_k L_l M_m N_n O_o P

1 3 5 7 9 11 13 15 17 19 21 23 25 27 29 31

Small Diamond Drop

5 Pegs
5 Inches of 18 or 20 Gauge Wire

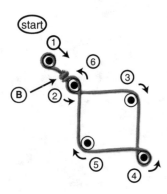

Bend wire here around chain nose pliers to form sharp 90 degree angle. Then place loop on jig. Black dots represent nose tips of the pliers.

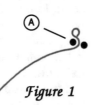

Figure 1

Tips: Form an eye loop in the wire. Place round nose pliers approximately 1/8 inch below the loop (*Figure 1*, **Arrow A**), and bend the wire 90 degrees around the nose of the pliers to form a right angle in the wire. Place the wire on the starting peg, and follow the arrows to form the design. To form a sharp angle at each of the side pegs, hold fingers close to the wire when wrapping around these pegs.

Remove the piece from the jig. Using bent chain nose pliers to hold the piece, wrap the wire tail around the neck of the starting loop (Arrow B) to finish.

To make an eye loop, see the section *"How to Make an Eye Loop"* in the *"Wire Working Tips & Hints"* chapter.

Variation: After completing the design, wrap a bead in wire, and attach it to the center loops as shown to the right.

For tips on attaching beads, see various techniques in the *"Wire Working Tips & Hints"* chapter.

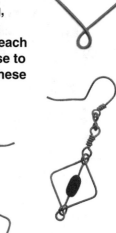

Reduced in Size

Note: Pegs placed inside the wire design(s) on this page have been slightly adjusted for illustrative purposes. Please copy the peg placements on the jig template when making the design(s).

WigJig Olympus Template

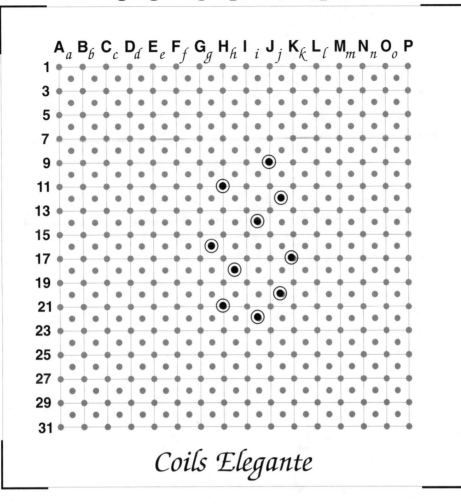

| | A | a | B | b | C | c | D | d | E | e | F | f | G | g | H | h | I | i | J | j | K | k | L | l | M | m | N | n | O | o | P |

Coils Elegante

10 Pegs
12 Inches of 18 Gauge Wire
14 Inches of 16 Gauge Wire

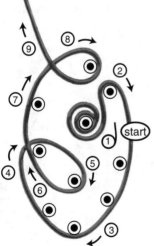

Tips: Form a scroll 1/2 inch in diameter in one end of the wire, being certain to leave the inside hole sized adequately to place over a peg. Forming the scroll will use approximately 2 to 3 inches of wire. Place the scroll on the starting peg as shown, and follow the arrows to form the design.

Remove the piece from the jig, and cut the wire 2 inches from the final wrap (last peg). Finish by forming a scroll using the remaining wire tail.

Reduced in Size

For tips on making scrolls and coils, see *"How to Make a Coil or Scroll"* in the *"Wire Working Tips & Hints"* chapter.

WigJig Olympus Template

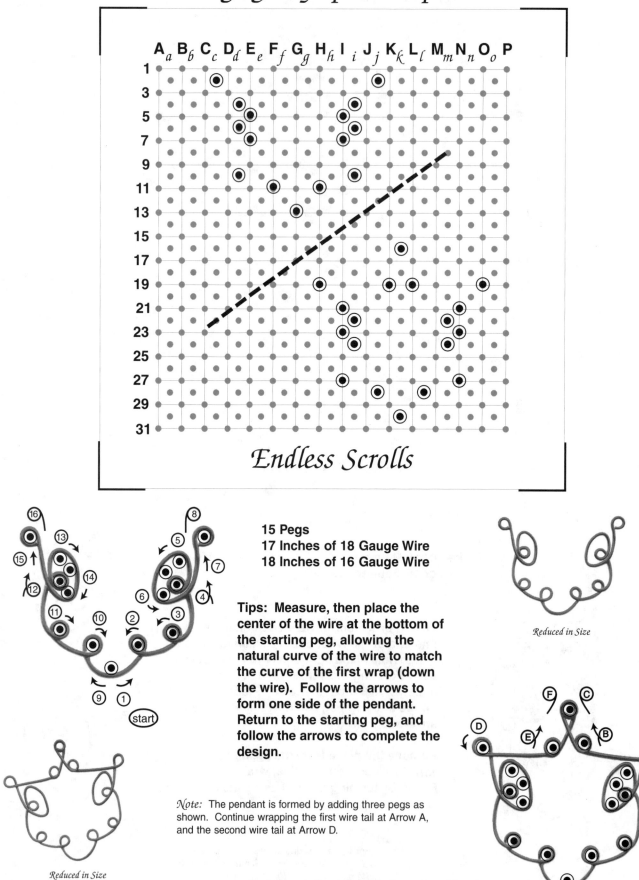

A B C D E F G H I J K L M N O P

Endless Scrolls

15 Pegs
17 Inches of 18 Gauge Wire
18 Inches of 16 Gauge Wire

Tips: Measure, then place the center of the wire at the bottom of the starting peg, allowing the natural curve of the wire to match the curve of the first wrap (down the wire). Follow the arrows to form one side of the pendant. Return to the starting peg, and follow the arrows to complete the design.

Reduced in Size

Note: The pendant is formed by adding three pegs as shown. Continue wrapping the first wire tail at Arrow A, and the second wire tail at Arrow D.

Reduced in Size

For tips on starting a design in the center of the wire, see *"How to Start at the Center of the Wire"* in the *"Wire Working Tips & Hints"* chapter.

WigJig Olympus Template

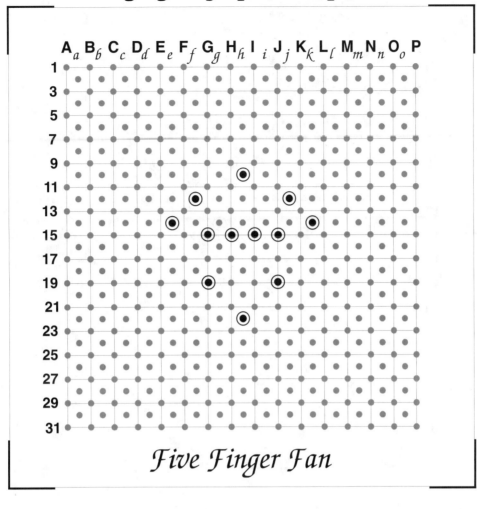

A$_a$ B$_b$ C$_c$ D$_d$ E$_e$ F$_f$ G$_g$ H$_h$ I $_i$ J$_j$ K$_k$ L$_l$ M$_m$ N$_n$ O$_o$ P

Five Finger Fan

12 Pegs
14 Inches of 18 Gauge Wire

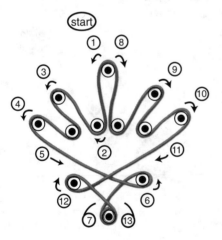

Tips: Measure, then place the center of the wire at the top of the starting peg, allowing the natural curve of the wire to match the curve of the first wrap (down the wire). Follow the arrows to form one side of the pendant. Return to the starting peg, and follow the arrows, completing the design.

For tips on starting a design in the center of the wire, see *"How to Start at the Center of the Wire"* in the *"Wire Working Tips & Hints"* chapter.

WigJig Olympus Template

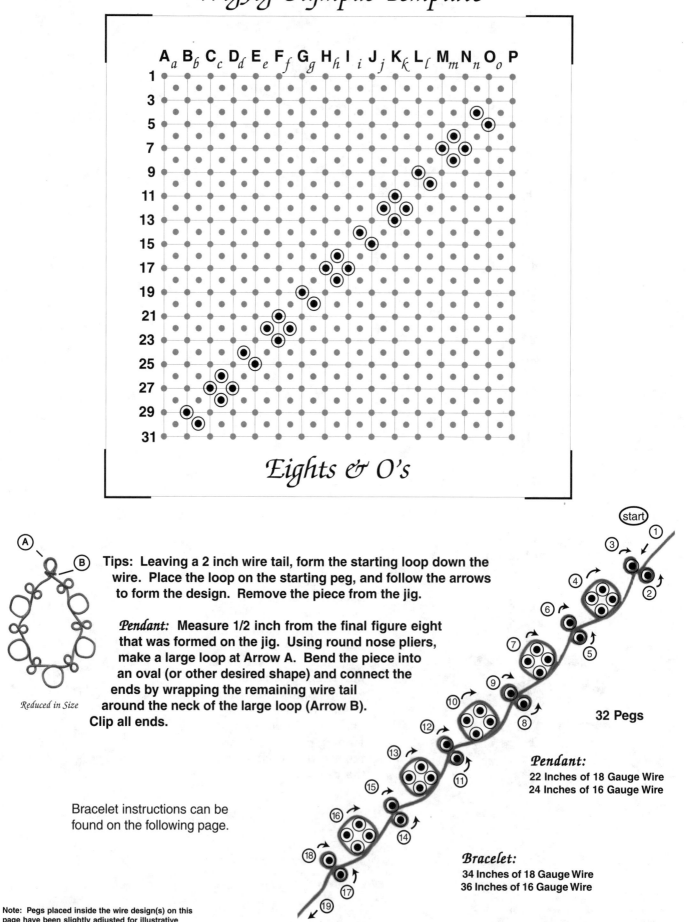

A B C D E F G H I J K L M N O P

Eights & O's

Tips: Leaving a 2 inch wire tail, form the starting loop down the wire. Place the loop on the starting peg, and follow the arrows to form the design. Remove the piece from the jig.

Pendant: Measure 1/2 inch from the final figure eight that was formed on the jig. Using round nose pliers, make a large loop at Arrow A. Bend the piece into an oval (or other desired shape) and connect the ends by wrapping the remaining wire tail around the neck of the large loop (Arrow B). Clip all ends.

Reduced in Size

Bracelet instructions can be found on the following page.

32 Pegs

Pendant:
22 Inches of 18 Gauge Wire
24 Inches of 16 Gauge Wire

Bracelet:
34 Inches of 18 Gauge Wire
36 Inches of 16 Gauge Wire

Note: Pegs placed inside the wire design(s) on this page have been slightly adjusted for illustrative purposes. Please copy the peg placements on the jig template when making the design(s).

Eights & O's *(Continued)*

Bracelet: After removing the piece from the jig, reposition it on the jig to wrap more loops in the pattern to the length desired (average length is 9 large loops and 9 figure eights). End the wrapping with a large loop.

Eye: Remove the piece from the jig, and wrap the ending wire tail around the neck of the final large loop. Clip end. This large loop will serve as the eye for the clasp.

Clasp: Using the remaining wire tail at the other end of the bracelet, form a tiny loop in the end of the wire (*Figure 1*, Arrow A). In *Figure 1*, the loop has been formed sideways for illustrative purposes only. It should be formed in direct line with the bracelet, as can be seen in *Figure 2*, Arrow C.

Grasp the wire tail below the tiny loop with round nose pliers, as shown (*Figure 1*, Arrow B). Bend the wire forward around the jaws of the pliers (*Figure 2*, Arrow D). This forms a clasp to hook into the eye of the bracelet. Note that the bend in the clasp around the pliers should be in the opposite direction of the curve of the tiny loop.

Figure 1

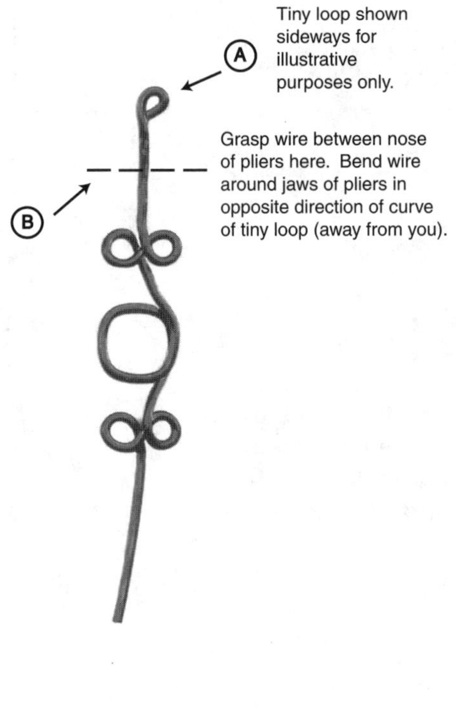

Tiny loop shown sideways for illustrative purposes only.

(A)

Grasp wire between nose of pliers here. Bend wire around jaws of pliers in opposite direction of curve of tiny loop (away from you).

(B)

Figure 2

(D) Bend in the wire around nose of pliers.

(C) Tiny loop finished correctly.

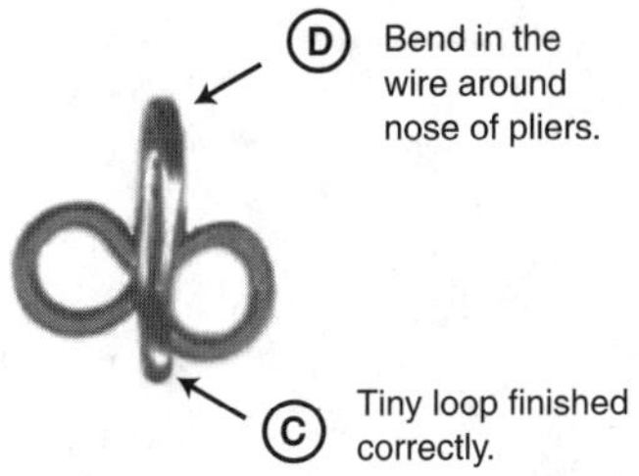

Enlarged to Show Detail

WigJig Olympus Template

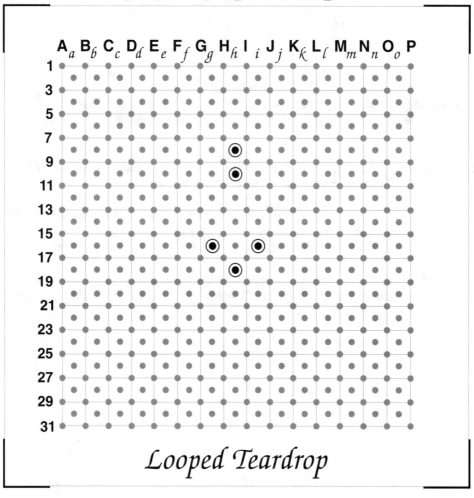

A_a B_b C_c D_d E_e F_f G_g H_h I_i J_j K_k L_l M_m N_n O_o P

1
3
5
7
9
11
13
15
17
19
21
23
25
27
29
31

Looped Teardrop

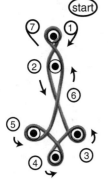

(start)

7   1
2   6
5   3
4

5 Pegs
8 Inches of 18 Gauge Wire

Tips: Form a loop up the wire. Place the loop on the starting peg, and follow the arrows to form the design.

Reduced in Size

Note: An expansion of this piece, called *"Snowflake"* can be found in the *"Sun Catchers & Holiday Ornaments"* chapter.

Note: Pegs placed inside the wire design(s) on this page have been slightly adjusted for illustrative purposes. Please copy the peg placements on the jig template when making the design(s).

WigJig Olympus Template

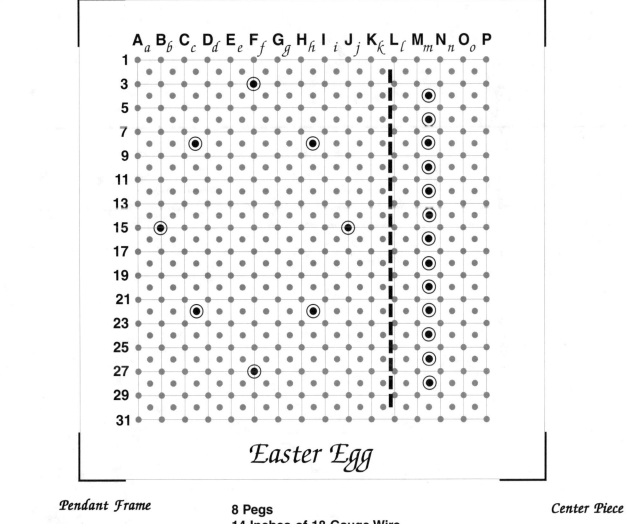

Easter Egg

Pendant Frame

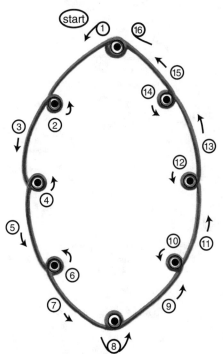

8 Pegs
14 Inches of 18 Gauge Wire
15 Inches of 16 Gauge Wire

Pendant Frame: Form a loop down the wire. Place the loop on the starting peg, and follow the arrows to form the pendant frame.

Center Piece: Form a loop down the wire. Place the loop on the starting peg, and follow the arrows to form the design.

Finishing: Join the center piece to the pendant at the top and bottom loops with a jump ring.

For tips on making jump rings, see *"How to Make Jump Rings"* in the *"Wire Working Tips & Hints"* chapter.

Center Piece

Reduced in Size

13 Pegs
12 Inches of 20 Gauge Wire
14 Inches of 18 Gauge Wire
15 Inches of 16 Gauge Wire

Note: Pegs placed inside the wire design(s) on this page have been slightly adjusted for illustrative purposes. Please copy the peg placements on the jig template when making the design(s).

WigJig Olympus Template

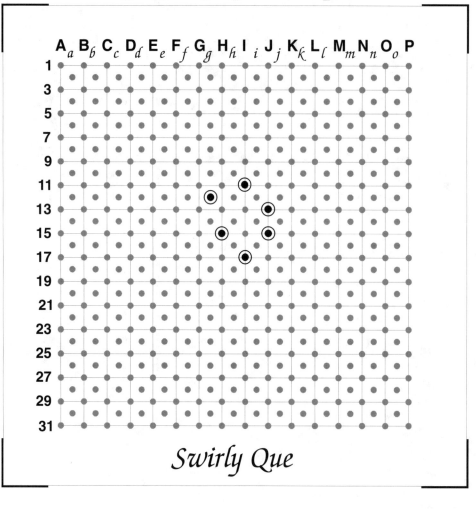

A a B b C c D d E e F f G g H h I i J j K k L l M m N n O o P

Swirly Que

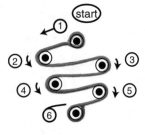

start
1
2 3
4 5
6

Reduced in Size

6 Pegs
5 Inches of 18 Gauge Wire

Tips: Form an eye loop in one end of the wire. (Option: Form eye loop 1 inch from end of wire. Then wrap wire tail around neck of eye loop to secure.) Place the eye loop on the starting peg, and follow the arrows to form the design. Hold fingers close to the pegs when wrapping. Use dowel to press the wire gently prior to removing from the jig *(Figure 1)*. Using an anvil and jeweler's hammer, firmly pound the design (with the exception of the eye loop and wrapped neck) to flatten *(Figure 2)*.

Variation: After hammering the piece, wrap a bead in wire, and attach it to the bottom loop as shown to the right.

Reduced in Size

Note: Pegs placed inside the wire design(s) on this page have been slightly adjusted for illustrative purposes. Please copy the peg placements on the jig template when making the design(s).

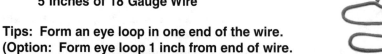

Figure 1

Figure 2

For tips on attaching beads, see the *"Wire Working Tips & Hints"* chapter.

To make an eye loop, see the section *"How to Make an Eye Loop"* in the *"Wire Working Tips & Hints"* chapter.

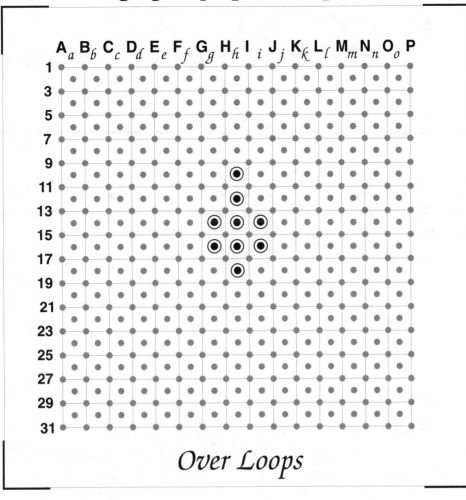

Over Loops

9 Pegs
9 Inches of 18 Gauge Wire

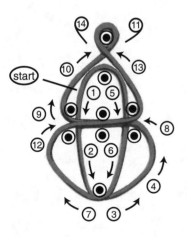

Enlarged to Show Detail

Tips: Measure the center of the wire, then press the center slightly around round nose pliers to form a bend in the wire. Place the bend above the starting peg, letting the natural curve of the wire follow the curve of the first wrap (down the wire). Wrap the first wire tail around the first three pegs through Arrow 4, then stop. Return to the starting peg and wrap the second wire tail through Arrow 7, then stop. Return to the first wire tail (Arrow 8, and continue wrapping through Arrow 11 at the ending peg. Return to the remaining wire tail (Arrow 12), and complete the design (through Arrow 14).

For tips on starting a design in the center of the wire, see *"How to Start at the Center of the Wire"* in the *"Wire Working Tips & Hints"* chapter.

Note: Pegs placed inside the wire design(s) on this page have been slightly adjusted for illustrative purposes. Please copy the peg placements on the jig template when making the design(s).

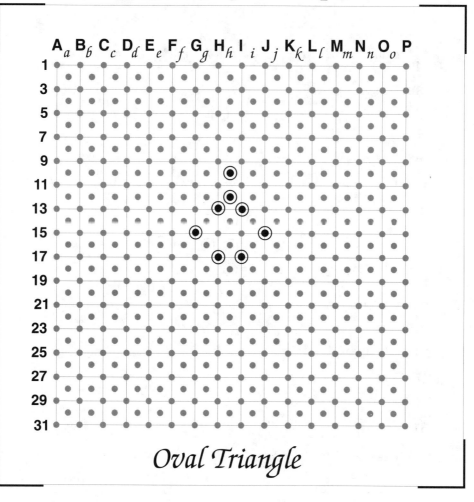

Oval Triangle

8 Pegs
9 Inches of 18 Gauge Wire

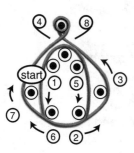

Tips: Measure, then place the center of the wire above the starting pegs, letting the natural curve of the wire follow the curve of the first wrap (down the wire). Wrap the first wire tail, following the arrows, as shown through Arrow 4. Return to the starting peg (Arrow 5), and fully wrap the remaining wire tail to finish the piece. Remove from the jig, and press into shape with fingers. Harden the wire, if necessary, to strengthen.

For tips on starting a design in the center of the wire, see *"How to Start at the Center of the Wire"* in the *"Wire Working Tips & Hints"* chapter.

Note: Pegs placed inside the wire design(s) on this page have been slightly adjusted for illustrative purposes. Please copy the peg placements on the jig template when making the design(s).

WigJig Olympus Template

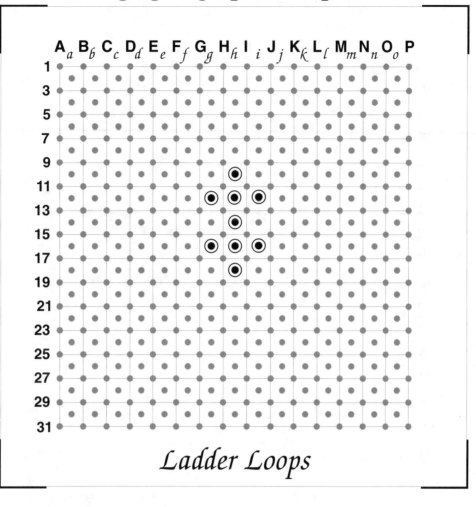

A _a_ B _b_ C _c_ D _d_ E _e_ F _f_ G _g_ H _h_ I _i_ J _j_ K _k_ L _l_ M _m_ N _n_ O _o_ P

1
3
5
7
9
11
13
15
17
19
21
23
25
27
29
31

Ladder Loops

9 Pegs
9 Inches of 18 Gauge Wire

Tips: Form a loop up the wire. Place the loop on the starting peg, and follow the arrows to form the design. Keep fingers close to the pegs while bending the wire. Flatten the wire with a metal dowel or other similar tool, and remove from the jig. Harden the wire by pressing with nylon jaw pliers or hammering lightly. Additionally, the top 3 loops can be secured in place using a binding wrap.

For tips on binding wire, see _"How to Bind the Wire"_ in the _"Wire Working Tips & Hints"_ chapter.

Note that there will be three loops around the top peg upon completion of the design.

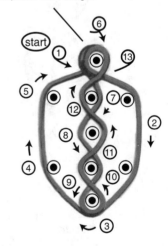

Enlarged to Show Detail

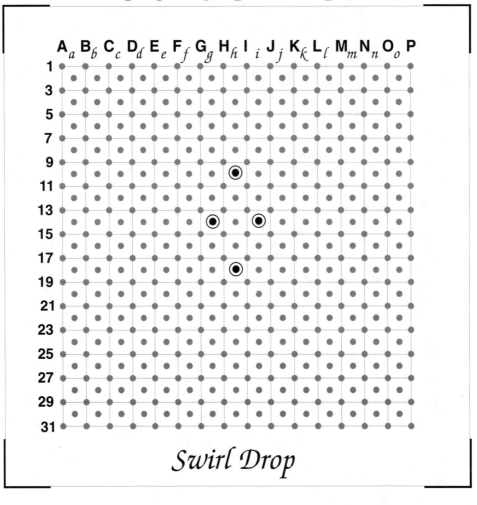

A_a B_b C_c D_d E_e F_f G_g H_h I_i J_j K_k L_l M_m N_n O_o P

Swirl Drop

4 Pegs
8 Inches of 18 Gauge Wire

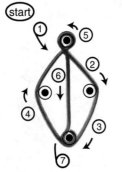

Tips: Form a loop up the wire. Place the loop on the starting peg, and follow the arrows to form the design.

Variation: After wrapping the top loop of the design, cut the wire tail 2-1/2 inches from the last peg. Remove the piece from the jig, and form a coil in the wire tail to the center of the piece, as shown to the left.

For tips on making scrolls and coils, see *"How to Make a Coil or Scroll"* in the *"Wire Working Tips & Hints"* chapter.

Variation (not shown): A bead can be added to the inside wire stem prior to wrapping the final loop.

Note: Pegs placed inside the wire design(s) on this page have been slightly adjusted for illustrative purposes. Please copy the peg placements on the jig template when making the design(s).

WigJig Olympus Template

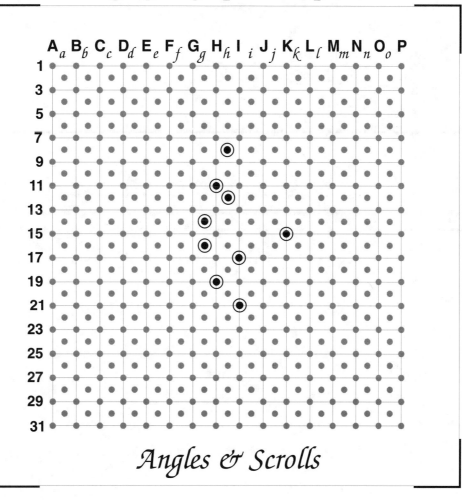

Angles & Scrolls

Reduced in Size

9 Pegs
8 Inches of 18 Gauge Wire
9 Inches of 16 Gauge Wire

Tips: Form a loop down the wire, then scroll slightly as shown in the drawing. Place the center of the wire scroll on the starting peg, and follow the arrows to form the design. Remove the piece from the jig.

To finish, wrap the wire tail around the neck of the piece twice (Arrow A). Adjust the starting loop slightly, if necessary.

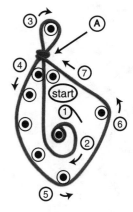

Note: Pegs placed inside the wire design(s) on this page have been slightly adjusted for illustrative purposes. Please copy the peg placements on the jig template when making the design(s).

WigJig Olympus Template

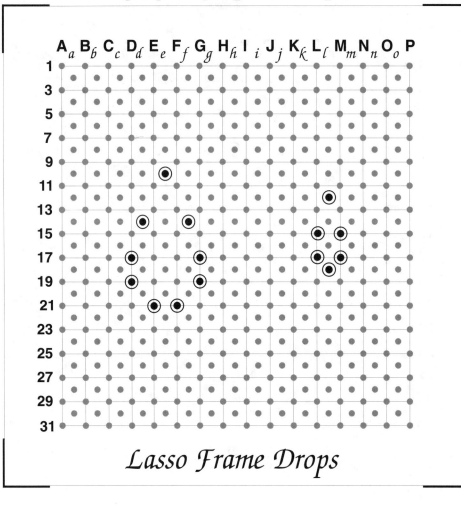

A_a B_b C_c D_d E_e F_f G_g H_h I_i J_j K_k L_l M_m N_n O_o P

Lasso Frame Drops

---

9 Pegs
5 Inches of 18 Gauge Wire

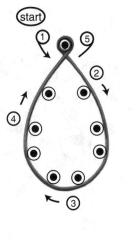

Tips: This earring design consists of two separate frames. Each is wrapped identically by forming a loop up the wire. Place the loop on the starting peg, and follow the arrows. Join the two frames with a figure eight loop.

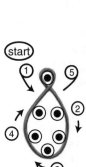

6 Pegs
4 Inches of 18 Gauge Wire

Reduced in Size

Variation: Instead of using the inner lasso frame, a bead can be incorporated into the design, as shown to the right.

For tips on making figure eight loops, see *"How to Make a Figure Eight Loop"* in the *"Wire Working Tips & Hints"* chapter.

Note: Pegs placed inside the wire design(s) on this page have been slightly adjusted for illustrative purposes. Please copy the peg placements on the jig template when making the design(s).

WigJig Olympus Template

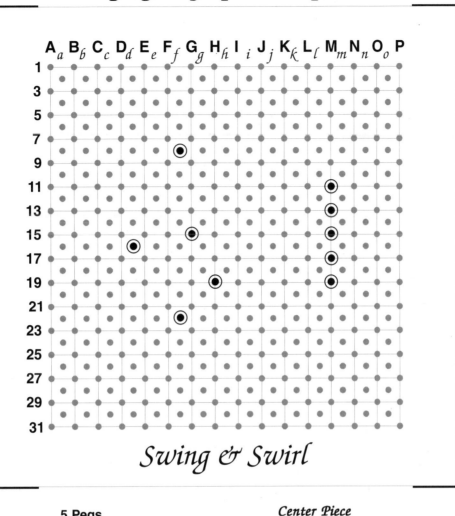

A_a B_b C_c D_d E_e F_f G_g H_h I_i J_j K_k L_l M_m N_n O_o P

Swing & Swirl

Earring Frame

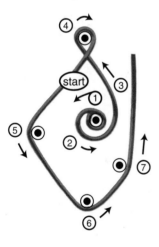

5 Pegs
8-1/2 Inches of 16 Gauge Wire

Earring Frame: Form a loop down the wire, then add the scroll as shown in the drawing. Place the wire scroll on the starting peg, and follow the arrows to form the earring. Clip the wire tail 1-1/2 inches from the last peg. Remove the piece from the jig, and form a loop in the end of the wire tail. Scroll the remaining wire tail. Curl the starting loop slightly, if necessary, to make the scrolls symmetrical. Gently press scrolls into place.

Center Piece

5 Pegs
4 Inches of 18 Gauge Wire

Center Piece: Using a new piece of wire, place a small loop at one end, and thread the bead onto the wire. Place the bead under the bottom peg on the jig, and follow the arrows to complete the design.

Finishing: **Complete the design by opening the top loop of the center piece and attaching it to the top loop of the earring frame. Adjust to allow the center piece to hang freely.**

Variation: The variation to the immediate right is formed by making larger scrolls and deleting the center piece.

Reduced in Size

Note: Pegs placed inside the wire design(s) on this page have been slightly adjusted for illustrative purposes. Please copy the peg placements on the jig template when making the design(s).

WigJig Olympus Template

	A a	B b	C c	D d	E e	F f	G g	H h	I i	J j	K k	L l	M m	N n	O o	P
1																

Rows labeled: 1, 3, 5, 7, 9, 11, 13, 15, 17, 19, 21, 23, 25, 27, 29, 31

Rounded Hearts

15 Pegs
8 Inches of 18 Gauge Wire

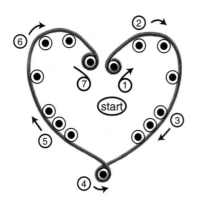

Tips: Form a loop down the wire. Place the loop on the starting peg, and follow the arrows to form the design.

Reduced in Size

Variation: The designs to the right show several variations that can be made using this same peg placement on the jig. The bottom peg can be wrapped in the opposite direction and beads can be added to the center of the heart for additional embellishment.

Note: Additional heart designs can be found in the *"Sun Catchers & Holiday Ornaments"* chapter.

WigJig Olympus Template

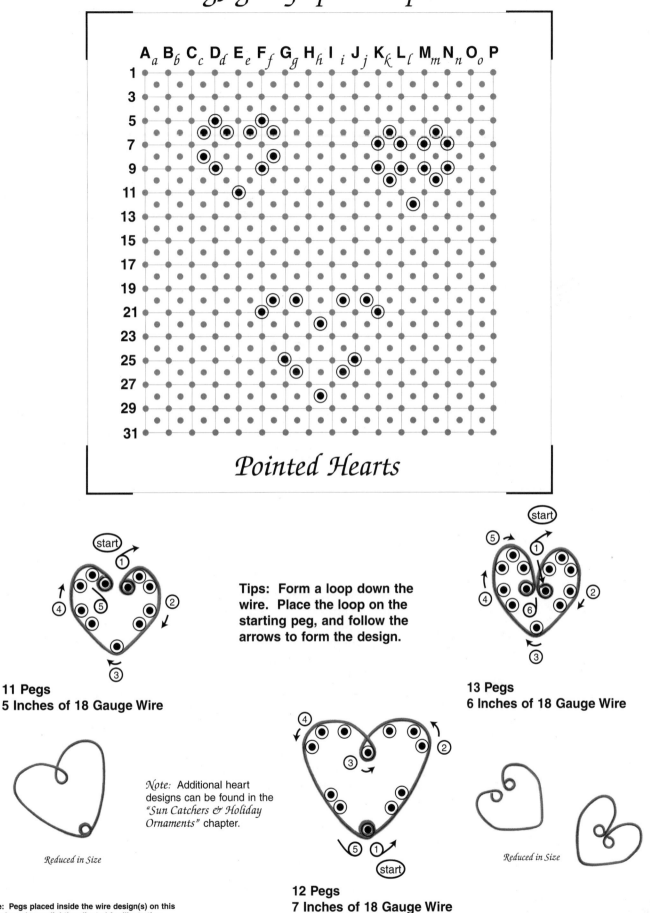

Pointed Hearts

Tips: Form a loop down the wire. Place the loop on the starting peg, and follow the arrows to form the design.

11 Pegs
5 Inches of 18 Gauge Wire

Reduced in Size

Note: Additional heart designs can be found in the *"Sun Catchers & Holiday Ornaments"* chapter.

13 Pegs
6 Inches of 18 Gauge Wire

Reduced in Size

12 Pegs
7 Inches of 18 Gauge Wire

WigJig Olympus Template

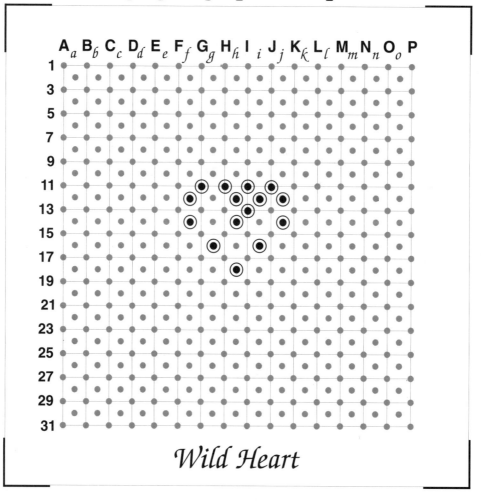

A a B b C c D d E e F f G g H h I i J j K k L l M m N n O o P

1
3
5
7
9
11
13
15
17
19
21
23
25
27
29
31

Wild Heart

15 Pegs
6 Inches of 18 Gauge Wire

Interim Piece

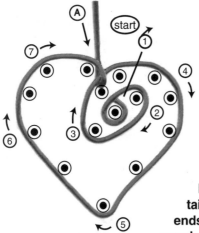

Enlarged to Show Detail

Tips: Form a loop down the wire. Place the loop on the starting peg, and follow the arrows to form the design. At the bottom peg (Arrow 5), hold fingers next to the peg, and bend the wire around and past the line of the design towards the side of the heart just formed. This will result in a sharp point at the bottom of the heart. Allow the wire to return to line of the design. Continue wrapping to complete. Remove the piece from the jig.

Hold the wire piece in place with bent chain nose pliers. Wrap the wire tail around the opposite half of the heart to close (Arrow A). Clip the ends to finish. Alternatively, prior to clipping the wire tail, a hanging loop may be added.

Note: Additional heart designs can be found in the *"Sun Catchers & Holiday Ornaments"* chapter.

Variation:: A variation of this piece as a pin can be found in the *"Yokes & Pins"* chapter.

Note: Pegs placed inside the wire design(s) on this page have been slightly adjusted for illustrative purposes. Please copy the peg placements on the jig template when making the design(s).

WigJig Olympus Template

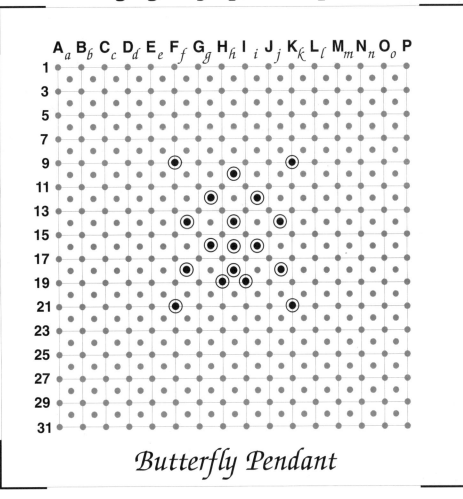

A a B b C c D d E e F f G g H h I i J j K k L l M m N n O o P

Butterfly Pendant

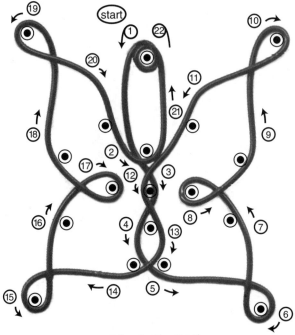

Enlarged to Show Detail

18 Pegs
15 Inches of 18 Gauge Wire

Tips: Form a loop down the wire. Place the loop on the starting peg, and follow the arrows to form the design. After completing the ending loop (Arrow 22), remove the piece from the jig.

To finish, twist the antennae around each other, and separate the loops.

Note: A large butterfly can be found in the *"Sun Catchers & Holiday Ornaments"* chapter.

Note: Pegs placed inside the wire design(s) on this page have been slightly adjusted for illustrative purposes. Please copy the peg placements on the jig template when making the design(s).

WigJig Olympus Template

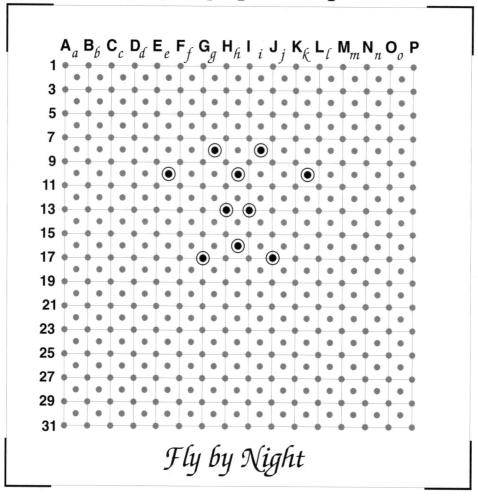

A B C D E F G H I J K L M N O P
a b c d e f g h i j k l m n o

1 3 5 7 9 11 13 15 17 19 21 23 25 27 29 31

Fly by Night

10 Pegs
12 Inches of 18 Gauge Wire
13 Inches of 16 Gauge Wire

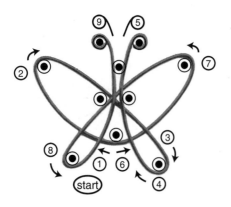

Tips: Measure and place the center of the wire below the starting peg, letting the natural curve of the wire follow the curve of the first wrap (down the wire). Wrap the first wire tail, following the arrows, as shown. Return to the starting peg and fully wrap the other wire tail to finish the piece.

For tips on starting a design in the center of the wire, see *"How to Start at the Center of the Wire"* in the *"Wire Working Tips & Hints"* chapter.

Note: A large butterfly can be found in the *"Sun Catchers & Holiday Ornaments"* chapter.

WigJig Olympus Template

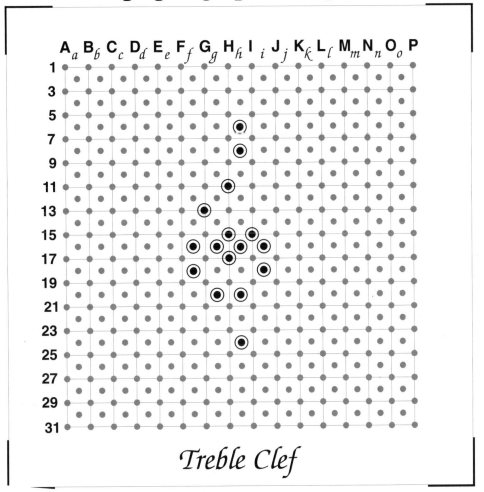

A_a B_b C_c D_d E_e F_f G_g H_h I_i J_j K_k L_l M_m N_n O_o P

Treble Clef

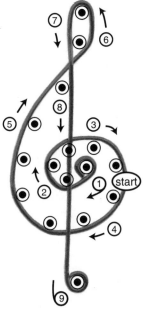

Enlarged to Show Detail

16 Pegs
10 Inches of 18 Gauge Wire

Tips: Form a loop down the wire.
Place the loop on the starting
peg, and follow the arrows to
form the design.

Reduced in Size

© 1998, Helwig Industries, LLC
& Karen Ray

(Page intentionally left blank)

Yokes
and
Pins

Wire designs in photograph on reverse side: Swirly S-Links (pg. 38), Petite Loops (pg. 103), Figure Eight Yoke (pg. 105), Classic Neck Piece (pg. 106), Hanging Loops (pg. 108), Scrolled Pin (pg. 116), and Heart to Heart (pg. 118).

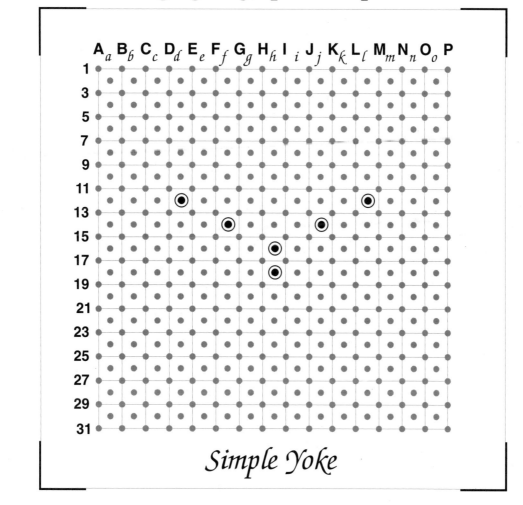

A_a B_b C_c D_d E_e F_f G_g H_h I_i J_j K_k L_l M_m N_n O_o P

Simple Yoke

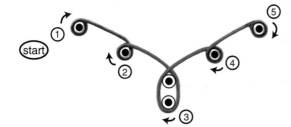

6 Pegs
6 Inches of 18 Gauge Wire (Yoke)
10 Inches of 18 Gauge Wire (Pin)

Yoke: Form a loop down the wire. Place the loop on the starting peg, and follow the arrows to form the design.

Pin: Form a double loop down the wire using round nose pliers. Place both loops on the starting peg, and follow the arrows to form the design. Wrap the last peg twice to form another double loop. Remove the piece from the jig. To finish, follow the directions in *"How to Make a Pin Using the Jig"* in the *"Wire Working Tips & Hints"* chapter.

WigJig Olympus Template

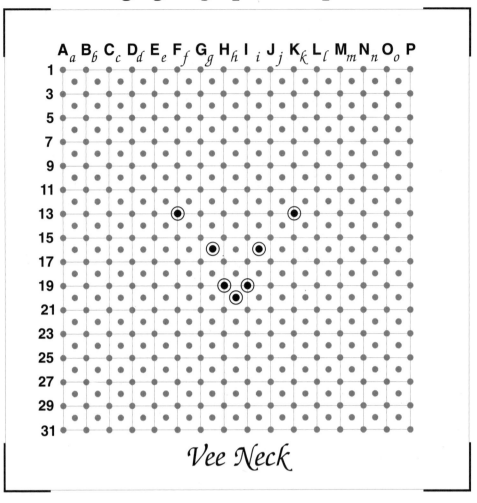

A B C D E F G H I J K L M N O P

1 3 5 7 9 11 13 15 17 19 21 23 25 27 29 31

Vee Neck

7 Pegs
7 Inches of 18 Gauge Wire

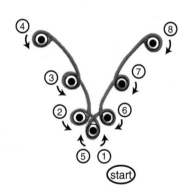

Tips: Measure, then place the center of the wire below the bottom peg, letting the natural curve of the wire follow the curve of the first wrap (down the wire). Wrap the first wire tail, following the arrows, as shown. Return to the starting peg, and fully wrap the other wire tail to finish the piece.

For tips on starting a design in the center of the wire, see *"How to Start at the Center of the Wire"* in the *"Wire Working Tips & Hints"* chapter.

WigJig Olympus Template

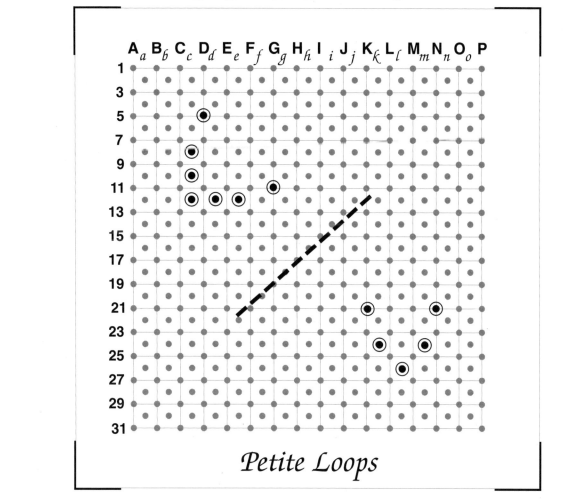

A_a B_b C_c D_d E_e F_f G_g H_h I_i J_j K_k L_l M_m N_n O_o P

1 3 5 7 9 11 13 15 17 19 21 23 25 27 29 31

Petite Loops

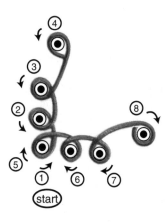

Enlarged to Show Detail

7 Pegs
7 Inches of 18 Gauge Wire
5-1/2 Inches of 20 Gauge Wire

Tips: For both designs, measure, then place the center of the wire below the starting peg, letting the natural curve of the wire follow the curve of the first wrap (down the wire). Wrap the first wire tail, following the arrows, as shown. Return to the starting peg and fully wrap the other wire tail to finish the piece.

Variation: The variation to the left is made by omitting two pegs at Arrows 3 and 7.

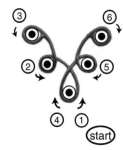

5 Pegs
4 Inches of 20 Gauge Wire

Reduced in Size

For tips on starting a design in the center of the wire, see *"How to Start at the Center of the Wire"* in the *"Wire Working Tips & Hints"* chapter.

WigJig Olympus Template

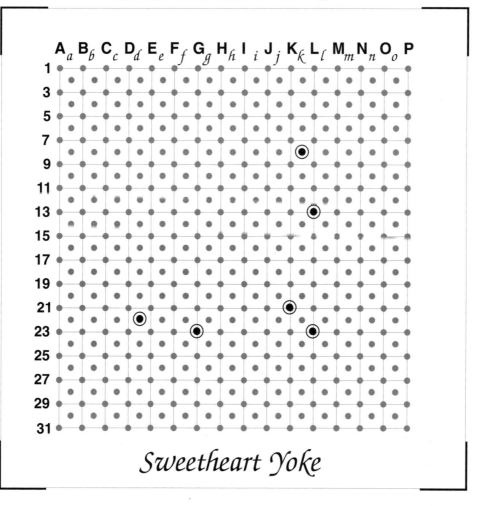

Sweetheart Yoke

6 Pegs
10 Inches of 16 Gauge Wire

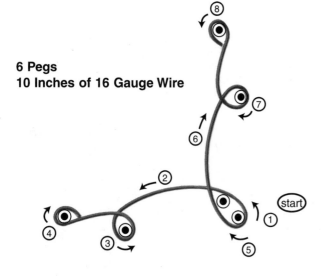

Tips: Measure, then place the center of the wire below the starting peg, letting the natural curve of the wire follow the curve of the first wrap (down the wire). Wrap the first wire tail, following the arrows, as shown. Return to the starting peg, and fully wrap the other wire tail to finish the piece.

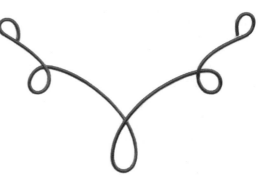

For tips on starting a design in the center of the wire, see *"How to Start at the Center of the Wire"* in the *"Wire Working Tips & Hints"* chapter.

WigJig Olympus Template

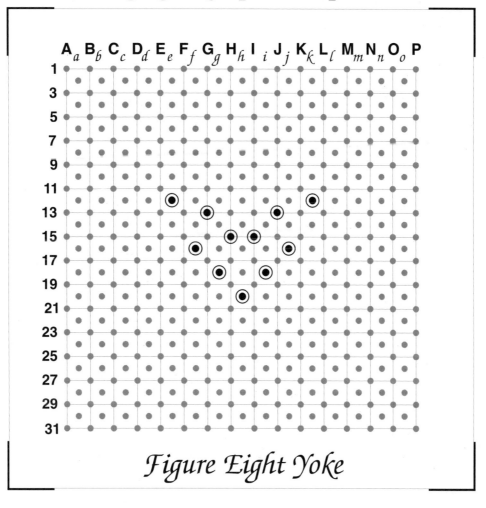

Figure Eight Yoke

11 Pegs
11 Inches of 20 Gauge Wire
11-1/2 Inches of 18 Gauge Wire
12 Inches of 16 Gauge Wire

Tips: Measure, then place the center of the wire below the bottom peg, placing the natural curve of the wire in the opposite direction of the curve of the first wrap (up the wire). Wrap the first wire tail, following the arrows, as shown. Return to the starting peg, and fully wrap the other wire tail to finish the piece.

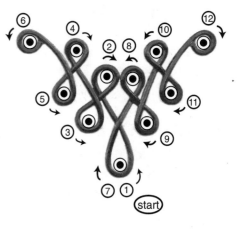

Enlarged to Show Detail

For tips on starting a design in the center of the wire, see *"How to Start at the Center of the Wire"* in the *"Wire Working Tips & Hints"* chapter.

WigJig Olympus Template

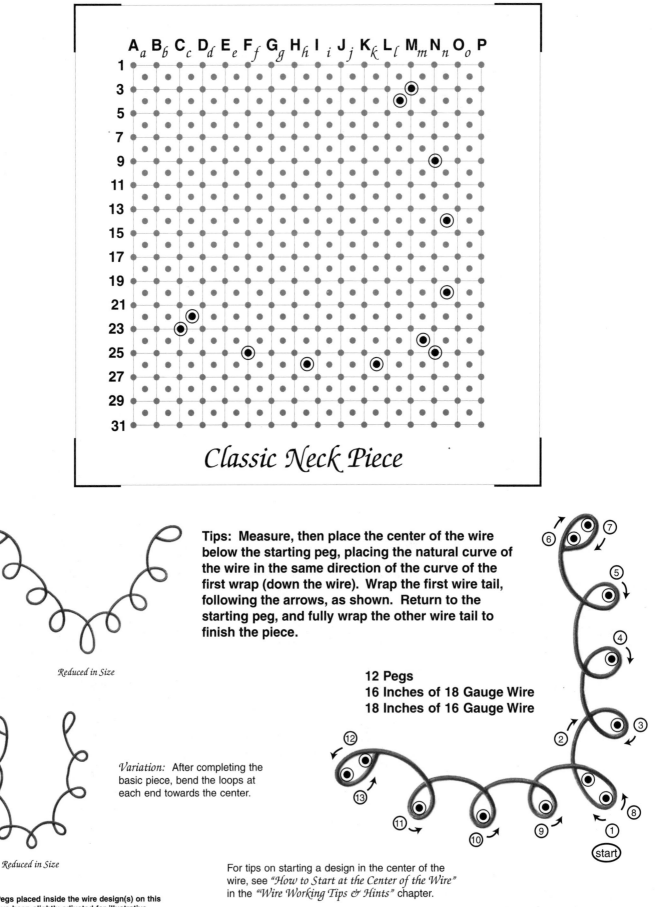

A a B b C c D d E e F f G g H h I i J j K k L l M m N n O o P

1 3 5 7 9 11 13 15 17 19 21 23 25 27 29 31

Classic Neck Piece

Reduced in Size

Tips: Measure, then place the center of the wire below the starting peg, placing the natural curve of the wire in the same direction of the curve of the first wrap (down the wire). Wrap the first wire tail, following the arrows, as shown. Return to the starting peg, and fully wrap the other wire tail to finish the piece.

12 Pegs
16 Inches of 18 Gauge Wire
18 Inches of 16 Gauge Wire

Variation: After completing the basic piece, bend the loops at each end towards the center.

Reduced in Size

For tips on starting a design in the center of the wire, see *"How to Start at the Center of the Wire"* in the *"Wire Working Tips & Hints"* chapter.

Note: Pegs placed inside the wire design(s) on this page have been slightly adjusted for illustrative purposes. Please copy the peg placements on the jig template when making the design(s).

WigJig Olympus Template

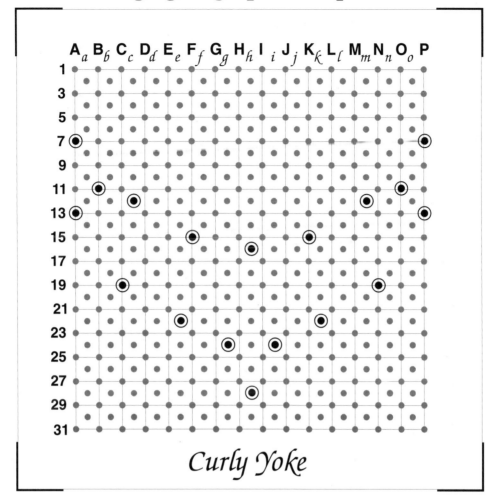

A_a B_b C_c D_d E_e F_f G_g H_h I_i J_j K_k L_l M_m N_n O_o P

Curly Yoke

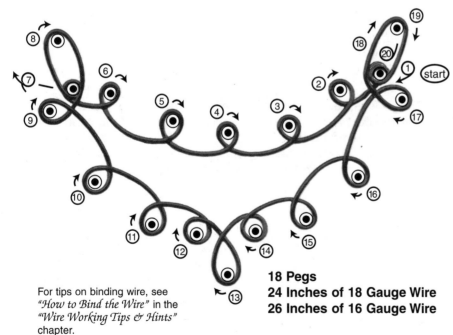

Tips: Form a loop down the wire. Place the loop on the starting peg, and follow the arrows to form the design.

Remove the wire piece from the jig, and intertwine the starting loop with the ending loop to close the piece. Alternatively, the starting and ending loops can be anchored using a binding wrap.

Reduced in Size

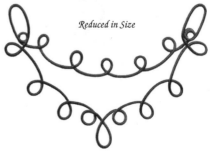

18 Pegs
24 Inches of 18 Gauge Wire
26 Inches of 16 Gauge Wire

For tips on binding wire, see *"How to Bind the Wire"* in the *"Wire Working Tips & Hints"* chapter.

Note: Pegs placed inside the wire design(s) on this page have been slightly adjusted for illustrative purposes. Please copy the peg placements on the jig template when making the design(s).

© 1998, Helwig Industries, LLC & Betty Bacon

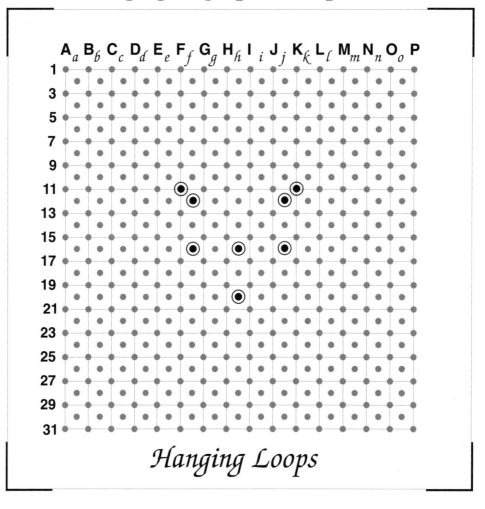

Hanging Loops

8 Pegs
8 Inches of 16 Gauge Wire

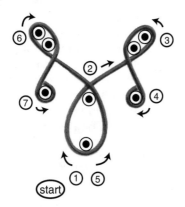

Tips: Measure, then place the center of the wire below the starting peg, letting the natural curve of the wire follow the curve of the first wrap (down the wire). Wrap the first wire tail, following the arrows, as shown. Return to the starting peg, and fully wrap the other wire tail to finish the piece.

For tips on starting a design in the center of the wire, see *"How to Start at the Center of the Wire"* in the *"Wire Working Tips & Hints"* chapter.

WigJig Olympus Template

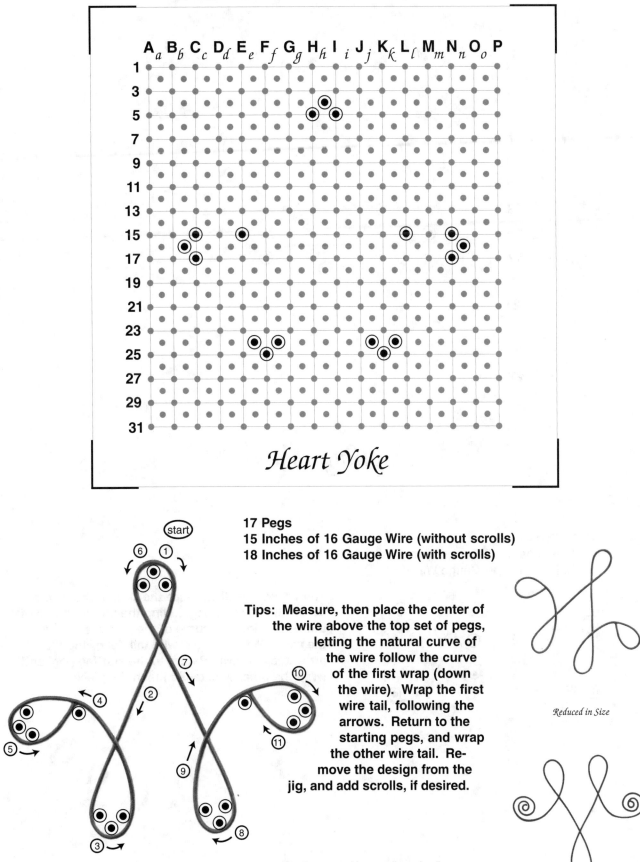

A B C D E F G H I J K L M N O P
1 3 5 7 9 11 13 15 17 19 21 23 25 27 29 31

Heart Yoke

17 Pegs
15 Inches of 16 Gauge Wire (without scrolls)
18 Inches of 16 Gauge Wire (with scrolls)

Tips: Measure, then place the center of the wire above the top set of pegs, letting the natural curve of the wire follow the curve of the first wrap (down the wire). Wrap the first wire tail, following the arrows. Return to the starting pegs, and wrap the other wire tail. Remove the design from the jig, and add scrolls, if desired.

Reduced in Size

For tips on making scrolls and coils, see *"How to Make a Coil or Scroll"* in the *"Wire Working Tips & Hints"* chapter.

Note: Pegs placed inside the wire design(s) on this page have been slightly adjusted for illustrative purposes. Please copy the peg placements on the jig template when making the design(s).

WigJig Olympus Template

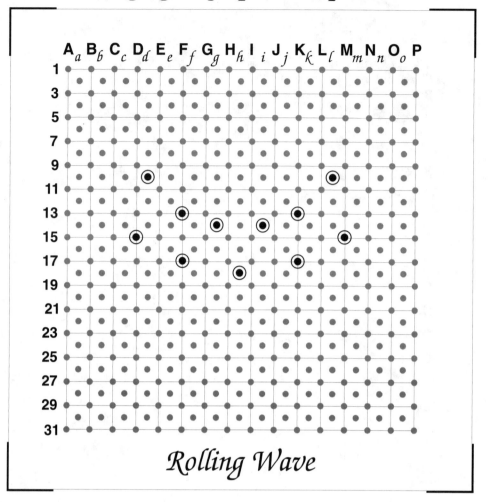

Rolling Wave

11 Pegs
12 Inches of 18 Gauge Wire
12 Inches of 16 Gauge Wire

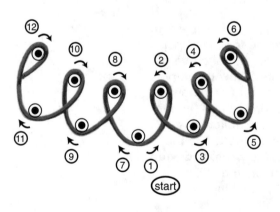

Tips: Measure, then place the center of the wire below the starting peg, letting the natural curve of the wire follow the curve of the first wrap (down the wire). Wrap the first wire tail, following the arrows, as shown. Return to the starting peg, and wrap the other wire tail to finish the piece.

For tips on starting a design in the center of the wire, see *"How to Start at the Center of the Wire"* in the *"Wire Working Tips & Hints"* chapter.

WigJig Olympus Template

A_a B_b C_c D_d E_e F_f G_g H_h I_i J_j K_k L_l M_m N_n O_o P

Five Fan Yoke

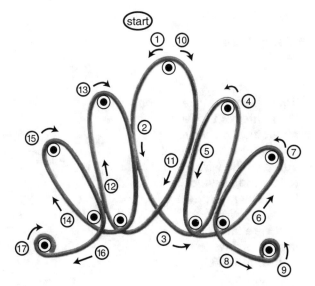

start

11 Pegs
14 Inches of 16 Gauge Wire

Tips: Measure, then place the center of the wire above the top center peg, letting the natural curve of the wire follow the curve of the first wrap (down the wire). Wrap the first wire tail, following the arrows. Return to the starting peg, and fully wrap the other wire tail to finish the piece.

Reduced in Size

For tips on starting a design in the center of the wire, see *"How to Start at the Center of the Wire"* in the *"Wire Working Tips & Hints"* chapter.

Note: Pegs placed inside the wire design(s) on this page have been slightly adjusted for illustrative purposes. Please copy the peg placements on the jig template when making the design(s).

WigJig Olympus Template

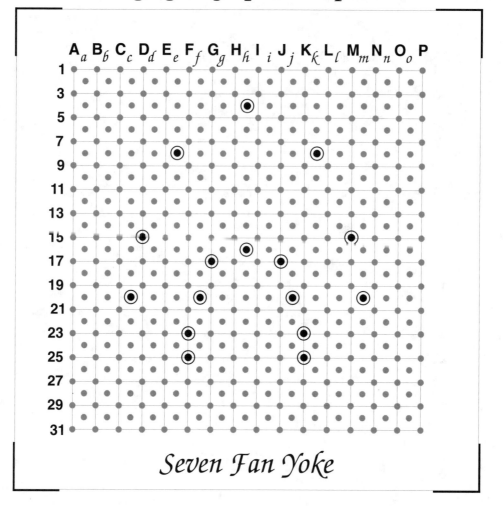

A a B b C c D d E e F f G g H h I i J j K k L l M m N n O o P

1 3 5 7 9 11 13 15 17 19 21 23 25 27 29 31

Seven Fan Yoke

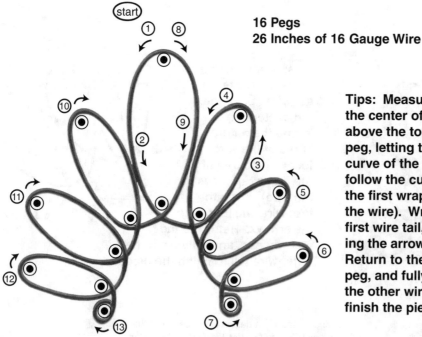

start

① ⑧
⑩ ④
⑨
② ⑤
③
⑪
⑥
⑫
⑬ ⑦

16 Pegs
26 Inches of 16 Gauge Wire

Tips: Measure, then place the center of the wire above the top center peg, letting the natural curve of the wire follow the curve of the first wrap (down the wire). Wrap the first wire tail, following the arrows. Return to the starting peg, and fully wrap the other wire tail to finish the piece.

Reduced in Size

For tips on starting a design in the center of the wire, see *"How to Start at the Center of the Wire"* in the *"Wire Working Tips & Hints"* chapter.

WigJig Olympus Template

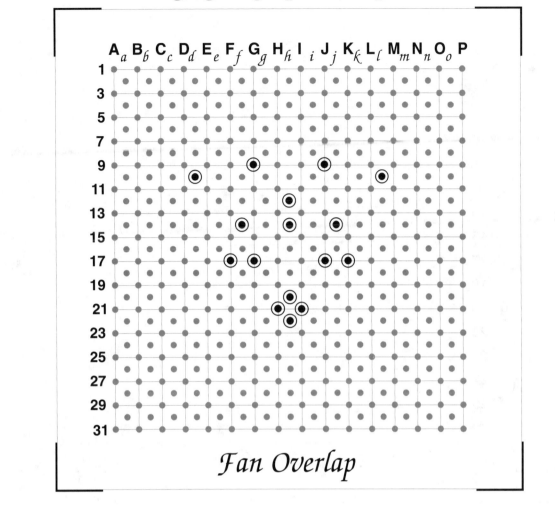

Fan Overlap

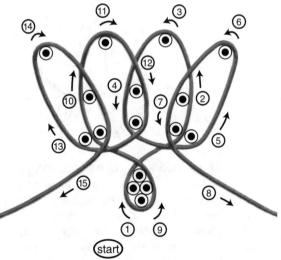

start

For tips on starting a design in the center of the wire, see *"How to Start at the Center of the Wire"* in the *"Wire Working Tips & Hints"* chapter.

Reduced in Size

16 Pegs
20 Inches of 16 Gauge Wire

Tips: Measure, then place the center of the wire below the bottom center set of pegs, letting the natural curve of the wire follow the curve of the first wrap (down the wire). Wrap the first wire tail, following the arrows. Return to the starting peg, wrap the other wire tail, and remove from jig. Clip wire tails to 3 inches in length. Form two coils to finish the piece.

For tips on making scrolls and coils, see *"How to Make a Coil or Scroll"* in the *"Wire Working Tips & Hints"* chapter.

WigJig Olympus Template

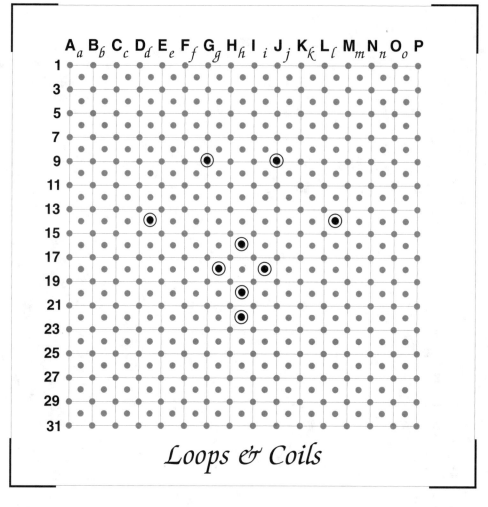

A_a B_b C_c D_d E_e F_f G_g H_h I_i J_j K_k L_l M_m N_n O_o P

1 3 5 7 9 11 13 15 17 19 21 23 25 27 29 31

Loops & Coils

9 Pegs
20 Inches of 16 Gauge Wire

Reduced in Size

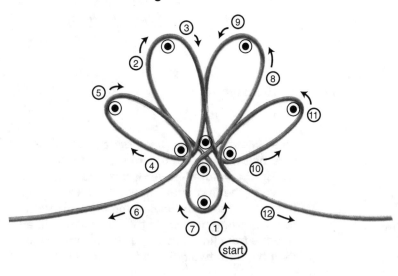

For tips on starting a design in the center of the wire, see *"How to Start at the Center of the Wire"* in the *"Wire Working Tips & Hints"* chapter.

Tips: Measure, then place the center of the wire below the bottom center peg, letting the natural curve of the wire follow the curve of the first wrap (down the wire). Wrap the first wire tail, following the arrows. Return to the starting peg, wrap the other wire tail, and remove from the jig. Allowing 3 inches of wire per scroll, coil each wire tail to finish the piece.

For tips on making scrolls and coils, see *"How to Make a Coil or Scroll"* in the *"Wire Working Tips & Hints"* chapter.

WigJig Olympus Template

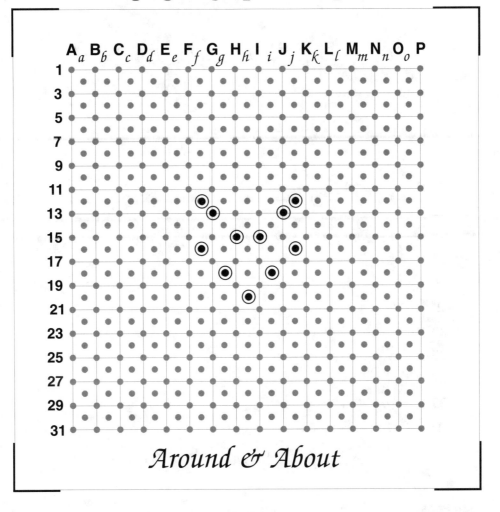

A B C D E F G H I J K L M N O P
a b c d e f g h i j k l m n o

1 3 5 7 9 11 13 15 17 19 21 23 25 27 29 31

Around & About

11 Pegs
14 Inches of 18 Gauge Wire

Tips: Leaving a 3-1/4 inch wire tail, place the wire on the starting peg, and follow the arrows to form the design. Remove the piece from the jig. Clip both wire tails to 3 inches in length. Form coils at each end. Be certain that the centers of the coils are adequately sized for connecting wire if the piece is to be attached to other components.

For tips on making scrolls and coils, see *"How to Make a Coil or Scroll"* in the *"Wire Working Tips & Hints"* chapter.

start
① ② ③ ④ ⑤ ⑥ ⑦ ⑧ ⑨ ⑩ ⑪

WigJig Olympus Template

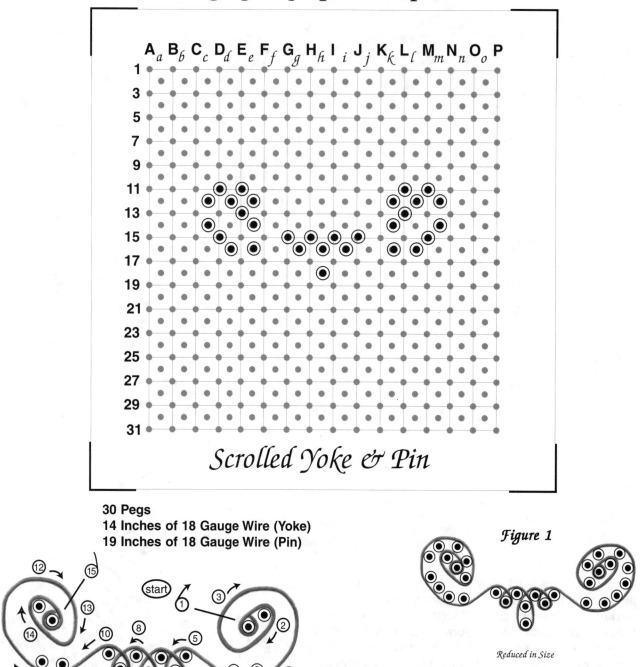

Scrolled Yoke & Pin

30 Pegs
14 Inches of 18 Gauge Wire (Yoke)
19 Inches of 18 Gauge Wire (Pin)

Enlarged to Show Detail

Figure 1

Reduced in Size

Note: Some pegs have been removed in the drawing to the left to provide adequate space for the arrows. *Figure 1* shows all the pegs in place.

Reduced in Size

Yoke: Form a loop down the wire. Place the loop on the starting peg, and follow the arrows to form the design.

Pin: Form a double loop down the wire using round nose pliers. Place both loops on the starting peg, and follow the arrows to form the design. Wrap the last peg twice to form another double loop. Remove the piece from the jig. To finish, follow the directions in *"How to Make a Pin Using the Jig"* in the *"Wire Working Tips & Hints"* chapter.

Note: Pegs placed inside the wire design(s) on this page have been slightly adjusted for illustrative purposes. Please copy the peg placements on the jig template when making the design(s).

© 1998, Helwig Industries, LLC & Karen Ray

116

WigJig Olympus Template

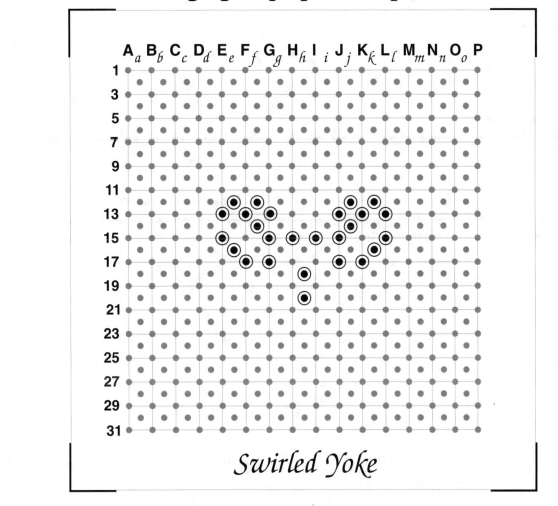

Swirled Yoke

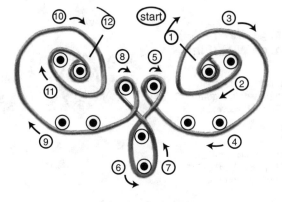

Enlarged to Show Detail

26 Pegs
13 Inches of 18 Gauge Wire (Yoke)
17 Inches of 18 Gauge Wire (Pin)

Note: Some pegs have been removed in the drawing to the left to provide adequate space for the arrows. *Figure 1* shows all the pegs in place.

Figure 1

Reduced in Size

Yoke: Form a loop down the wire. Place the loop on the starting peg, and follow the arrows to form the design.

Pin: Form a double loop down the wire using round nose pliers. Place both loops on the starting peg, and follow the arrows to form the design. Wrap the last peg twice to form another double loop. Remove the piece from the jig. To finish, follow the directions in *"How to Make a Pin Using the Jig"* in the *"Wire Working Tips & Hints"* chapter.

Reduced in Size

Note: Pegs placed inside the wire design(s) on this page have been slightly adjusted for illustrative purposes. Please copy the peg placements on the jig template when making the design(s).

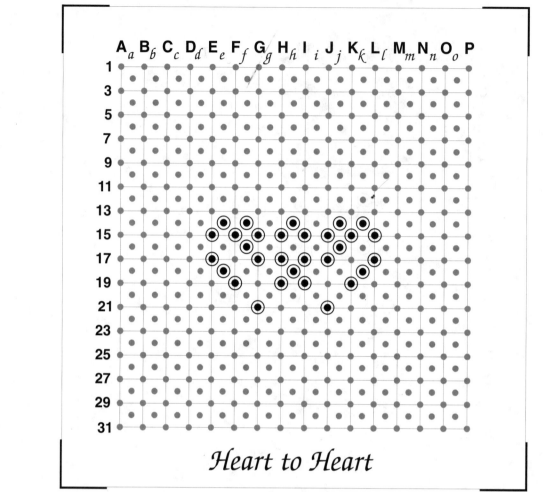

Heart to Heart

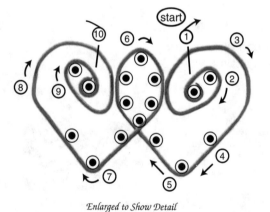

start
10 6 1
8   3
9   2
7   5 4

Enlarged to Show Detail

30 Pegs
13 Inches of 18 Gauge Wire (Yoke)
17 Inches of 18 Gauge Wire (Pin)

Note: Some pegs have been removed in the drawing to the left to provide adequate space for the arrows. *Figure 1* shows all the pegs in place.

Note: Additional heart designs can be found in the *"Sun Catchers & Holiday Ornaments"* and *"Pendants & Earrings"* chapters.

Figure 1

Yoke: Form a loop down the wire. Place the loop on the starting peg, and follow the arrows to form the design.

Pin: Approximately 1/2 inch from the end, form a double loop down the wire using round nose pliers. Place both loops on the starting peg, and follow the arrows to form the design. Wrap the last peg twice to form another double loop. Remove the piece from the jig. To finish, follow the directions in *"How to Make a Pin Using the Jig"* in the *"Wire Working Tips & Hints"* chapter.

Note: Pegs placed inside the wire design(s) on this page have been slightly adjusted for illustrative purposes. Please copy the peg placements on the jig template when making the design(s).

WigJig Olympus Template

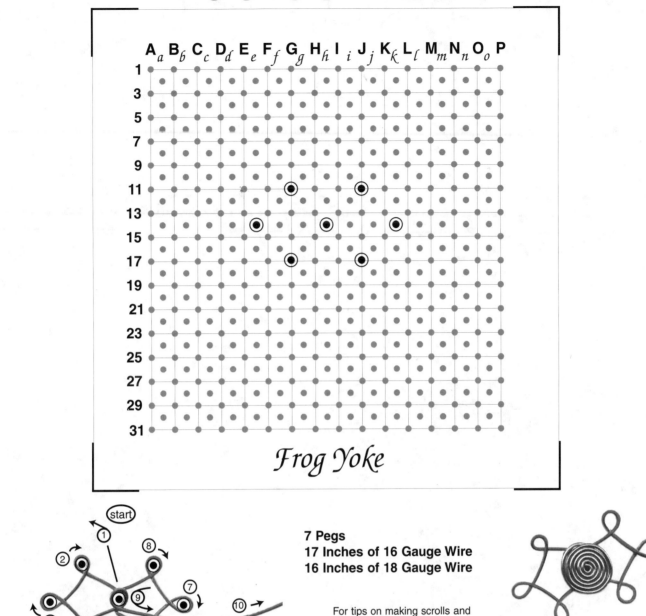

A_a B_b C_c D_d E_e F_f G_g H_h I_i J_j K_k L_l M_m N_n O_o P

Frog Yoke

7 Pegs
17 Inches of 16 Gauge Wire
16 Inches of 18 Gauge Wire

Actual wire tail will be longer

For tips on making scrolls and coils, see *"How to Make a Coil or Scroll"* in the *"Wire Working Tips & Hints"* chapter.

Reduced in Size

Tips: Make a loop down the wire, place it on the center peg and follow the arrows. Note that the center peg will have 3 loops after completion of the design. Remove the piece from the jig.

Wrap the wire tail several times around the middle of the piece to secure. Alternatively, the three center loops can be anchored in place using a binding wrap. To finish, coil the end of the wire tail (approximately 6 inches) towards the center of the piece. Adjust the coil over the top of the piece as shown.

Variation: The variation to the right can be made by ending at the second wrap of the center peg (Arrow 5), and removing the piece from the jig. Clip the wire tail to 6 inches and coil.

Reduced in Size

For tips on binding wire, see *"How to Bind the Wire"* in the *"Wire Working Tips & Hints"* chapter.

Note: Pegs placed inside the wire design(s) on this page have been slightly adjusted for illustrative purposes. Please copy the peg placements on the jig template when making the design(s).

© 1998, Helwig Industries, LLC & Betty Bacon

119

(Page intentionally left blank)

Wire designs in photograph on reverse side: Heart to Heart (pg. 118), Singing in the Rain (pg. 133), Contrite Angel (pg. 138), and Holly Leaves (pg. 141).

WigJig Olympus Template

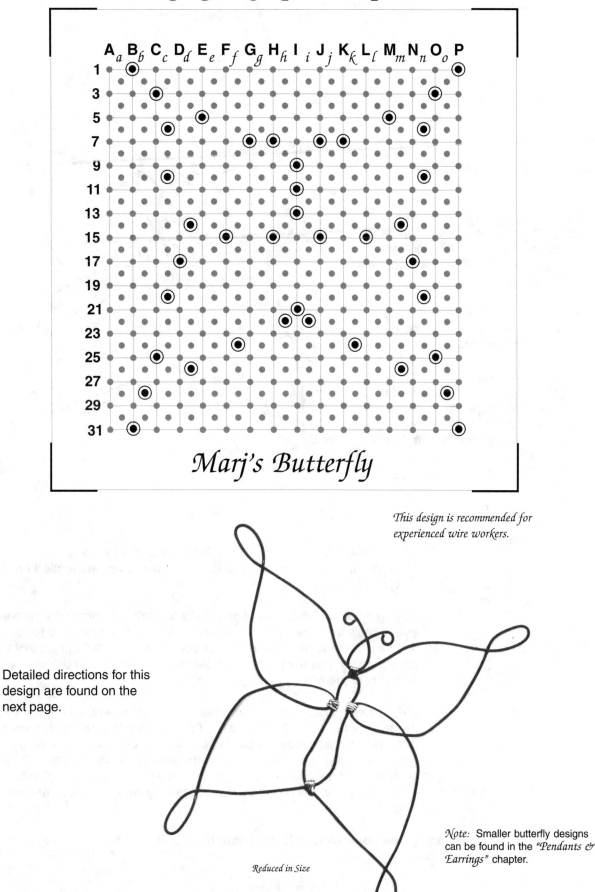

Marj's Butterfly

This design is recommended for experienced wire workers.

Detailed directions for this design are found on the next page.

Reduced in Size

Note: Smaller butterfly designs can be found in the *"Pendants & Earrings"* chapter.

Marj's Butterfly (continued)

Figure 1

40 Pegs
30 inches of 18 Gauge Wire

(1) Form a loop down the wire. Place the loop on the starting peg, and follow the arrows to form the design. Remove the piece from the jig *(Figure 1)*.

(2) Squeeze the butterfly's body where the wings meet the body *(Figure 2*, Arrow A).

(3) Bind the butterfly's body together at Arrows B, C, D, and E, in that order *(Figure 2)*. Prior to binding at Arrow E, hook the right antenna under the left antenna.

Figure 2

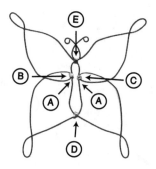

Reduced in Size

Binding Instructions: Cut a 4 inch piece of 22 or 24 gauge wire for each of the four bindings (half round wire is recommended for this type of wrap).

Using small round-nosed pliers, make a small loop down the wire in the end of the wire. The loop should be the size of the wire used to form the butterfly. (If using half round wire, make certain that the flat side of the wire is on the inside of the loop.) Hook this loop around the back of the butterfly at the binding site.

Grip the wire firmly with chain nose pliers, and wrap the wire tightly around the butterfly. Press the binding wire firmly with chain nose pliers after each wrap to lock the wire into place. Grasp the wire wrap again with chain nose pliers and wrap tightly around the back of the piece and again around the front. Again, press firmly with chain nose pliers. Repeat to form a minimum of three tight wraps around the body, ending on the back of the piece. Clip the wire tail of the binding wire.

In order to achieve a neat, professional wrap, it is important to stop at each turn, and press the wire firmly with chain nose pliers.

Note: Pegs placed inside the wire designs on this page have been slightly adjusted for illustrative purposes. Please copy the peg placements on the jig template when making this design.

For more tips on binding wire, see *"How to Bind the Wire"* in the *"Wire Working Tips & Hints"* chapter.

WigJig Olympus Template

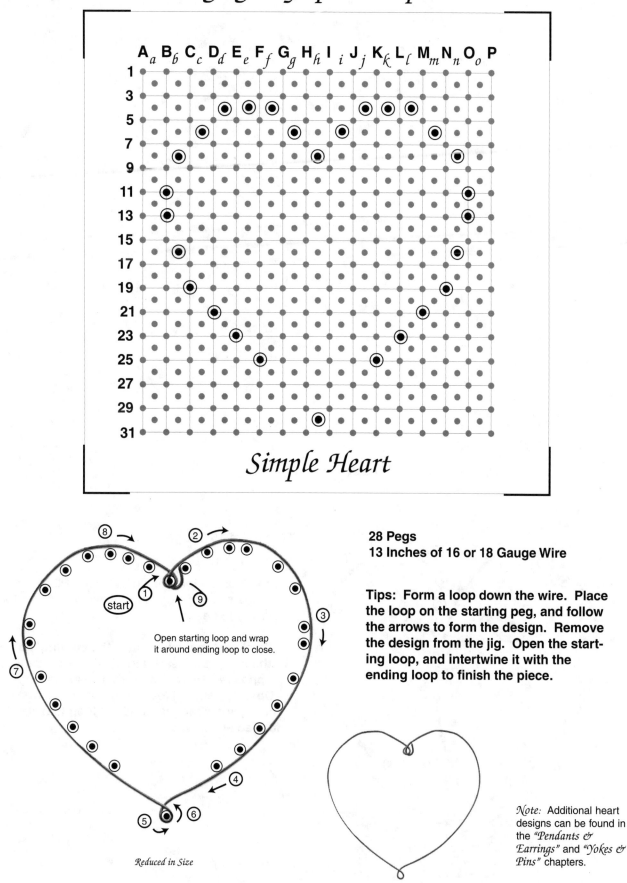

A_a B_b C_c D_d E_e F_f G_g H_h I_i J_j K_k L_l M_m N_n O_o P

1 3 5 7 9 11 13 15 17 19 21 23 25 27 29 31

Simple Heart

28 Pegs
13 Inches of 16 or 18 Gauge Wire

start

Open starting loop and wrap
it around ending loop to close.

Tips: Form a loop down the wire. Place
the loop on the starting peg, and follow
the arrows to form the design. Remove
the design from the jig. Open the starting loop, and intertwine it with the
ending loop to finish the piece.

Reduced in Size

Note: Additional heart
designs can be found in
the *"Pendants &
Earrings"* and *"Yokes &
Pins"* chapters.

Reduced in Size

Note: Pegs placed inside the wire design(s) on this
page have been slightly adjusted for illustrative
purposes. Please copy the peg placements on the jig
template when making the design(s).

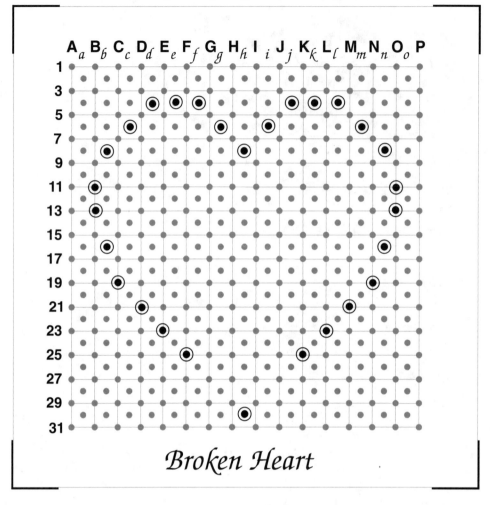

Broken Heart

28 Pegs
17 Inches of 16 Gauge Wire

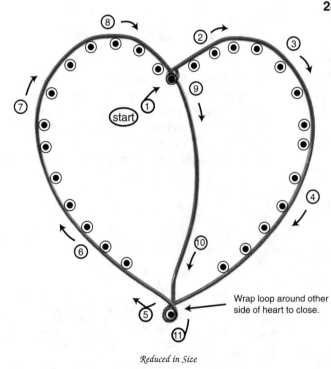

Reduced in Size

Wrap loop around other side of heart to close.

Tips: Form a loop down the wire. Place the loop on the starting peg, and follow the arrows to form the design.

To close the design, open the starting loop at the top of the heart and wrap it around the opposite side of the heart. Close the loop. Open the ending loop at the bottom of the heart, and wrap it around the loop that was formed at Arrow 5.

Reduced in Size

Note: Additional heart designs can be found in the *"Pendants & Earrings"* and *"Yokes & Pins"* chapters.

Note: Pegs placed inside the wire design(s) on this page have been slightly adjusted for illustrative purposes. Please copy the peg placements on the jig template when making the design(s).

WigJig Olympus Template

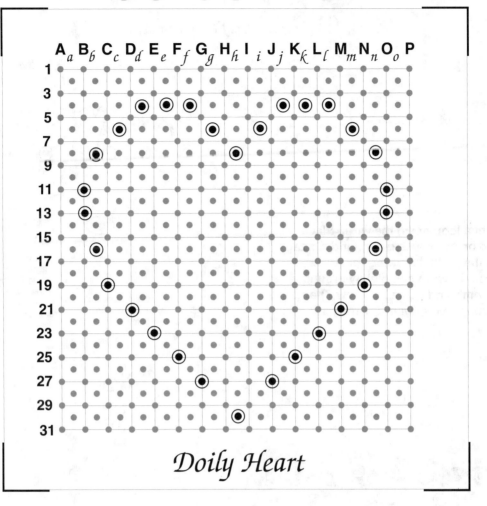

Doily Heart

Detailed directions for this design are found on the next page.

Note: Additional heart designs can be found in the *"Pendants & Earrings"* and *"Yokes & Pins"* chapters.

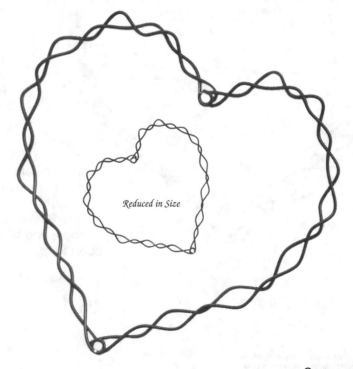

Reduced in Size

Note: Pegs placed inside the wire design(s) on this page have been slightly adjusted for illustrative purposes. Please copy the peg placements on the jig template when making the design(s).

Doily Heart *(continued)*

Figure 1

30 Pegs
27 Inches of 18 Gauge Wire

(1) Form a loop down the wire. Place the loop on the starting peg, and zig zag around the pegs, following the arrows. Be certain to wrap completely around the bottom peg (*Figure 1,* Arrow 7) and the starting peg (*Figure 1,* Arrow 15).

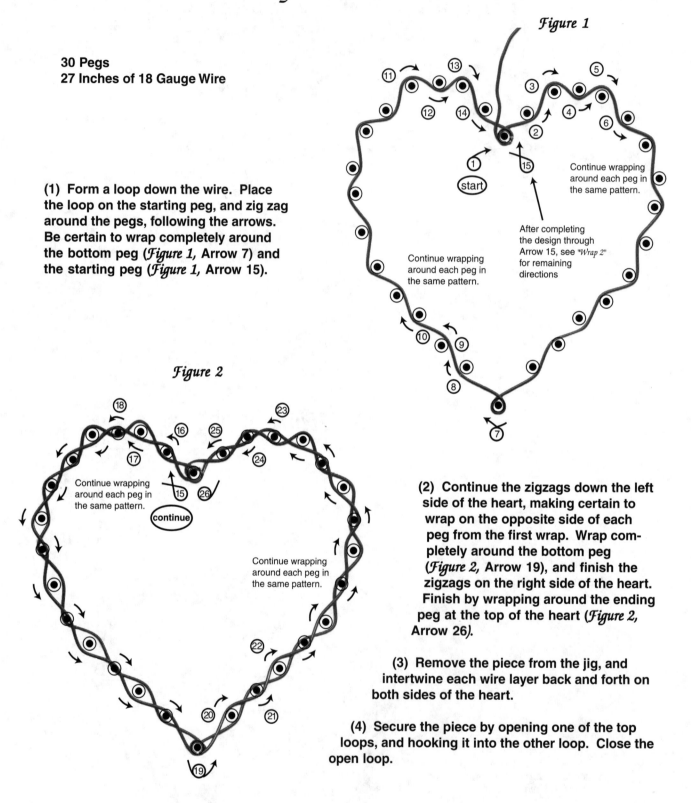

Continue wrapping around each peg in the same pattern.

After completing the design through Arrow 15, see *"Wrap 2"* for remaining directions

Continue wrapping around each peg in the same pattern.

Figure 2

Continue wrapping around each peg in the same pattern.

Continue wrapping around each peg in the same pattern.

(2) Continue the zigzags down the left side of the heart, making certain to wrap on the opposite side of each peg from the first wrap. Wrap completely around the bottom peg (*Figure 2,* Arrow 19), and finish the zigzags on the right side of the heart. Finish by wrapping around the ending peg at the top of the heart (*Figure 2,* Arrow 26).

(3) Remove the piece from the jig, and intertwine each wire layer back and forth on both sides of the heart.

(4) Secure the piece by opening one of the top loops, and hooking it into the other loop. Close the open loop.

Note: Pegs placed inside the wire designs on this page have been slightly adjusted for illustrative purposes. Please copy the peg placements on the jig template when making this design.

WigJig Olympus Template

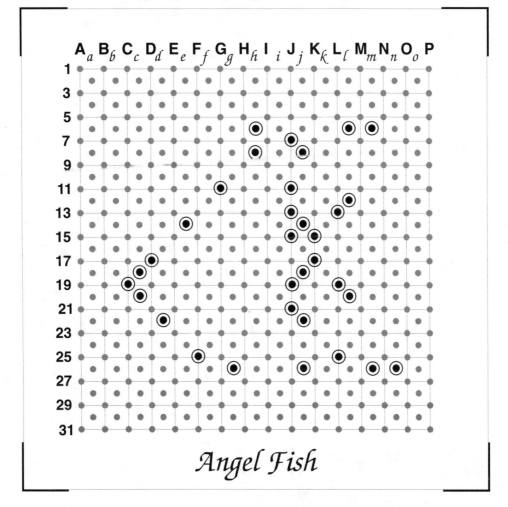

A a B b C c D d E e F f G g H h I i J j K k L l M m N n O o P

Angel Fish

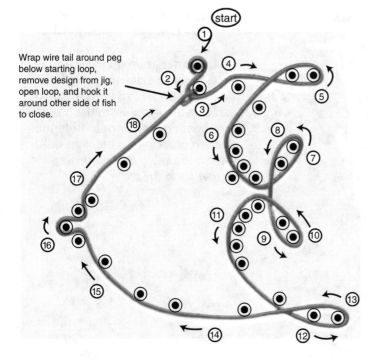

Wrap wire tail around peg below starting loop, remove design from jig, open loop, and hook it around other side of fish to close.

33 Pegs
17 Inches of 16 Gauge Wire

Tips: Form a loop up the wire. Place the loop on the starting peg, and follow the arrows to form the design. Before removing the piece from the jig, wrap the remaining wire tail around the peg located below the starting peg. Remove the piece from the jig, clip the wire tail, open the ending loop, and hook it around the other side of the piece, as shown.

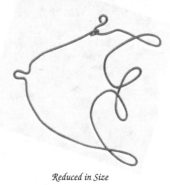

Reduced in Size

WigJig Olympus Template

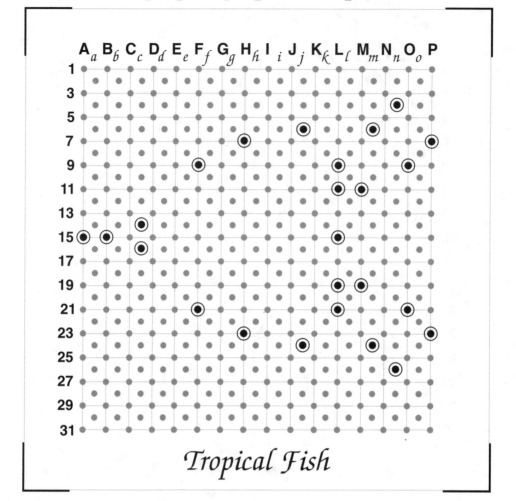

Tropical Fish

25 Pegs
20 Inches of 18 Gauge Wire

Tips: Form a loop up the wire. Place the loop on the starting peg, and follow the arrows to form the design. Remove the piece from the jig. Using bent chain nose pliers to hold the piece in place, wrap the wire tail around the neck of the starting loop (Arrow A) to finish.

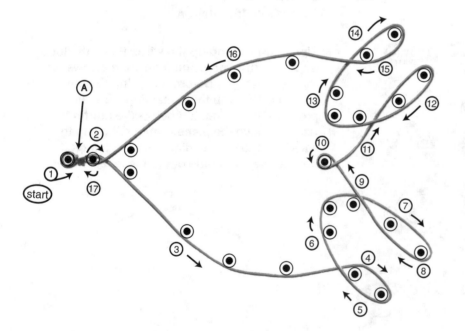

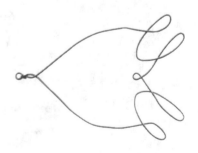

Reduced in Size

Note: Pegs placed inside the wire design(s) on this page have been slightly adjusted for illustrative purposes. Please copy the peg placements on the jig template when making the design(s).

WigJig Olympus Template

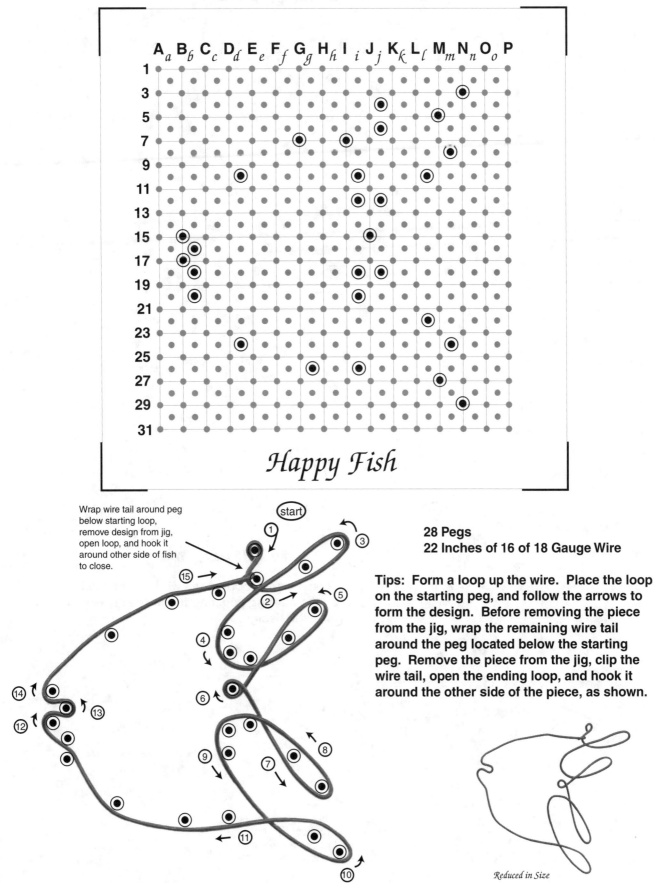

A a B b C c D d E e F f G g H h I i J j K k L l M m N n O o P

1 3 5 7 9 11 13 15 17 19 21 23 25 27 29 31

Happy Fish

Wrap wire tail around peg below starting loop, remove design from jig, open loop, and hook it around other side of fish to close.

start

28 Pegs
22 Inches of 16 of 18 Gauge Wire

Tips: Form a loop up the wire. Place the loop on the starting peg, and follow the arrows to form the design. Before removing the piece from the jig, wrap the remaining wire tail around the peg located below the starting peg. Remove the piece from the jig, clip the wire tail, open the ending loop, and hook it around the other side of the piece, as shown.

Reduced in Size

Note: Pegs placed inside the wire design(s) on this page have been slightly adjusted for illustrative purposes. Please copy the peg placements on the jig template when making the design(s).

WigJig Olympus Template

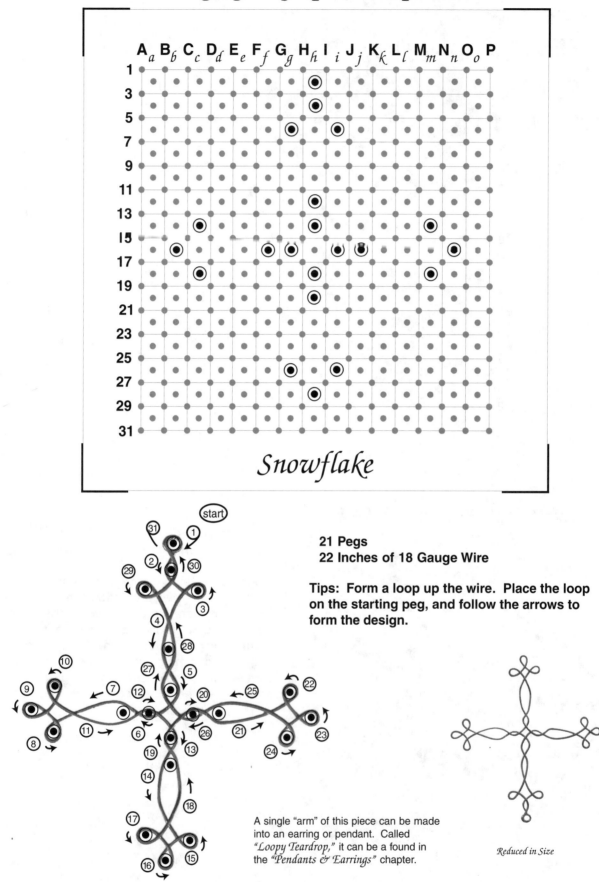

Snowflake

21 Pegs
22 Inches of 18 Gauge Wire

Tips: Form a loop up the wire. Place the loop on the starting peg, and follow the arrows to form the design.

A single "arm" of this piece can be made into an earring or pendant. Called *"Loopy Teardrop,"* it can be a found in the *"Pendants & Earrings"* chapter.

Reduced in Size

WigJig Olympus Template

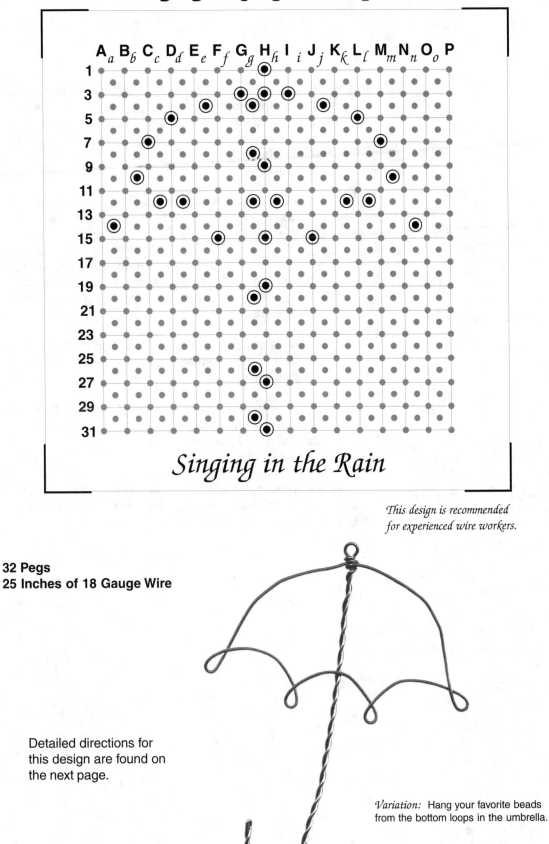

Singing in the Rain

This design is recommended for experienced wire workers.

32 Pegs
25 Inches of 18 Gauge Wire

Detailed directions for this design are found on the next page.

Variation: Hang your favorite beads from the bottom loops in the umbrella.

Reduced in Size

Figure 1 *Singing in the Rain* (continued)

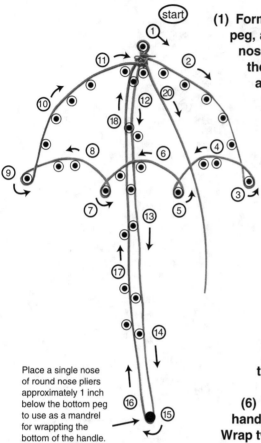

(1) Form an eye loop in the wire. Place the loop on the starting peg, and wrap through Arrow 14 *(Figure 1)*. Place a single nose of round nose pliers 1 inch below the bottom peg on the jig, wrap around the nose *(Figure 1,* Arrows 15 and 16*)*, and continue, through Arrow 18. Remove the design from the jig.

(2) Using a vise (recommended) or chain nose pliers, grasp the starting loop, the base of the wire tail, and the top of the wire handle *(Figure 2)*.

(3) Insert a dowel in the loop at the bottom tip of the handle, and turn until a uniform twist is obtained in the wires of the umbrella handle. Remove the dowel *(Figure 2)*.

(4) Squeeze the sides of the loop at the bottom of the handle together. Twist the wire to match the uniform twist formed in step (3).

(5) Bend the bottom of the umbrella handle around a mandrel (pen, dowel, or finger), and form a half loop in the handle *(Figure 3)*.

(6) Wrap the remaining wire tail once around the umbrella handle underneath the umbrella cover *(Figure 4,* Arrow B). Wrap twice around the handle above the umbrella cover *(Figure 4,* Arrow C) to complete the design.

Place a single nose of round nose pliers approximately 1 inch below the bottom peg to use as a mandrel for wrappting the bottom of the handle.

Reduced in Size

Figure 2

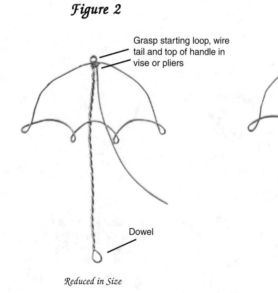

Grasp starting loop, wire tail and top of handle in vise or pliers

Dowel

Reduced in Size

Figure 3

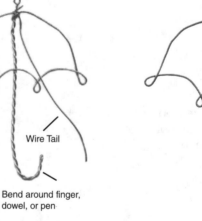

Wire Tail

Bend around finger, dowel, or pen

Reduced in Size

Figure 4

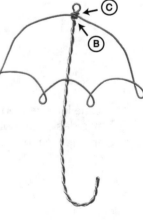

Reduced in Size

Note: Pegs placed inside the wire designs on this page have been slightly adjusted for illustrative purposes. Please copy the peg placements on the jig template when making this design.

WigJig Olympus Template

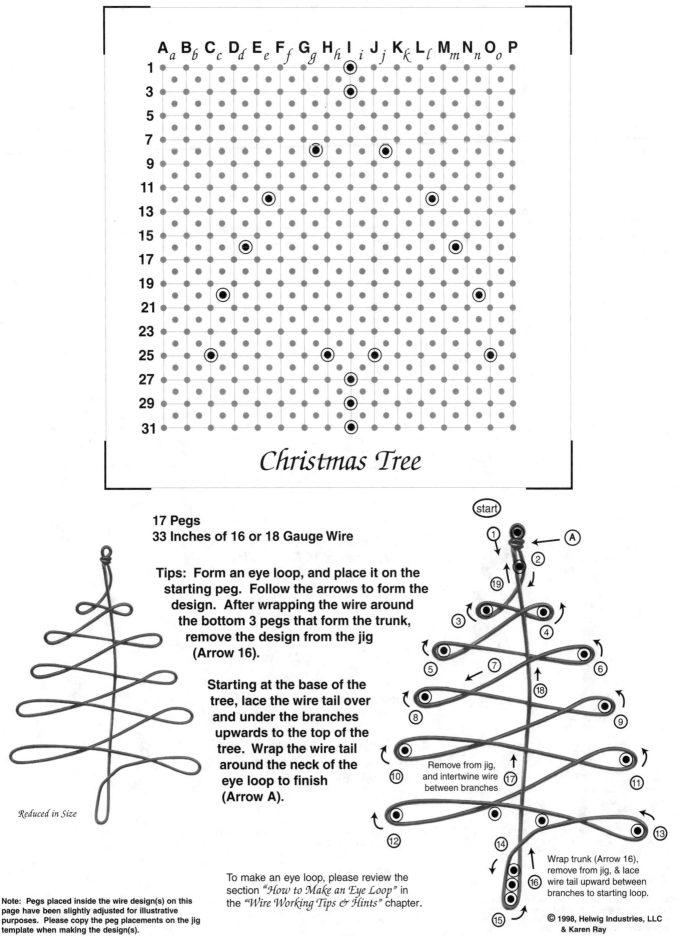

A_a B_b C_c D_d E_e F_f G_g H_h I_i J_j K_k L_l M_m N_n O_o P

Christmas Tree

17 Pegs
33 Inches of 16 or 18 Gauge Wire

Tips: Form an eye loop, and place it on the starting peg. Follow the arrows to form the design. After wrapping the wire around the bottom 3 pegs that form the trunk, remove the design from the jig (Arrow 16).

Starting at the base of the tree, lace the wire tail over and under the branches upwards to the top of the tree. Wrap the wire tail around the neck of the eye loop to finish (Arrow A).

Reduced in Size

start

A

Remove from jig, and intertwine wire between branches

Wrap trunk (Arrow 16), remove from jig, & lace wire tail upward between branches to starting loop.

To make an eye loop, please review the section *"How to Make an Eye Loop"* in the *"Wire Working Tips & Hints"* chapter.

WigJig Olympus Template

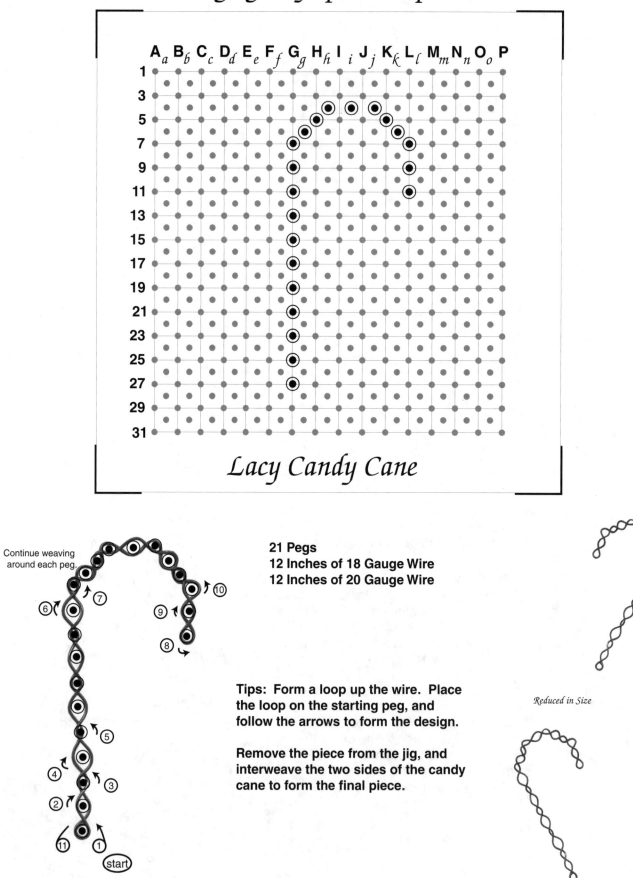

Lacy Candy Cane

Continue weaving around each peg.

21 Pegs
12 Inches of 18 Gauge Wire
12 Inches of 20 Gauge Wire

Tips: Form a loop up the wire. Place the loop on the starting peg, and follow the arrows to form the design.

Remove the piece from the jig, and interweave the two sides of the candy cane to form the final piece.

Reduced in Size

Note: Pegs placed inside the wire design(s) on this page have been slightly adjusted for illustrative purposes. Please copy the peg placements on the jig template when making the design(s).

WigJig Olympus Template

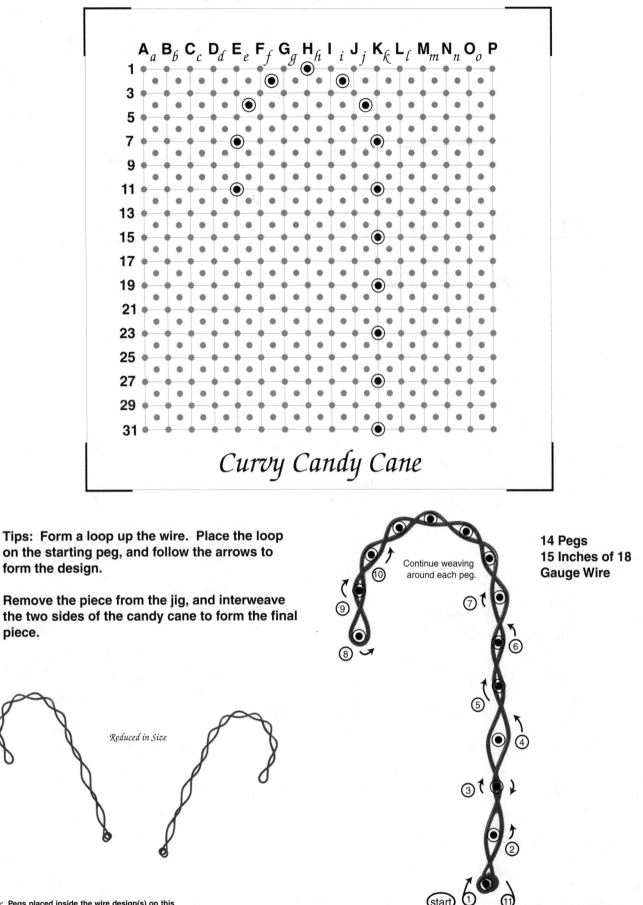

Curvy Candy Cane

Tips: Form a loop up the wire. Place the loop on the starting peg, and follow the arrows to form the design.

Remove the piece from the jig, and interweave the two sides of the candy cane to form the final piece.

Continue weaving around each peg.

14 Pegs
15 Inches of 18
Gauge Wire

Reduced in Size

Note: Pegs placed inside the wire design(s) on this page have been slightly adjusted for illustrative purposes. Please copy the peg placements on the jig template when making the design(s).

WigJig Olympus Template

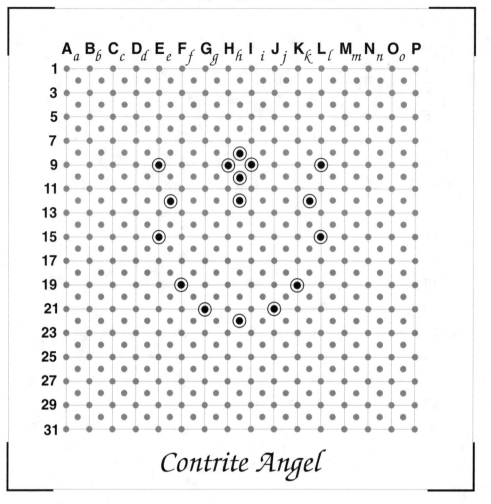

Contrite Angel

This design is recommended for experienced wire workers.

16 Pegs
19 Inches of 18 Gauge Wire

Directions for this design are found on the next page.

Note: Finished design includes a halo (not shown).

Figure 1

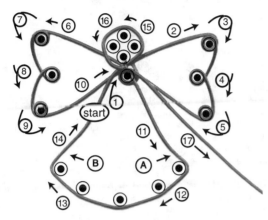

(1) Form a large loop down the wire. Place the loop on the starting peg, and follow the arrows to form the design. When wrapping around the pegs at Arrows A and B, pinch the wire around each peg to form a flair in the skirt (*Figure 1*).

(2) Remove the piece from the jig.

(3) Open the starting loop and close the wing piece and skirt in the loop (*Figure 2*).

(4) Wrap the wire tail around the angel's body between the wings 1-1/2 times, ending on the back of the piece (*Figure 2*).

(5) Bend the wire sharply on the back of the piece so that the wire tail points vertically upward, behind the angel's head (*Figure 2*).

(6) Approximately 1/8 inch above the angel's head, grip the wire tail using round nose pliers (*Figure 2*). Bend the wire tail forward around the nose of the pliers to form a 90 degree angle. In other words, when holding the angel facing forward in front of you, the bent wire tail will be pointing directly at you (*Figure 2*).

Figure 2

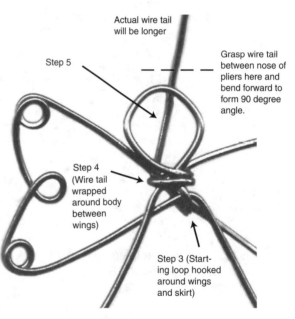

Actual wire tail will be longer

Step 5

Grasp wire tail between nose of pliers here and bend forward to form 90 degree angle.

Step 4 (Wire tail wrapped around body between wings)

Step 3 (Starting loop hooked around wings and skirt)

Enlarged to Show Detail

Figure 3

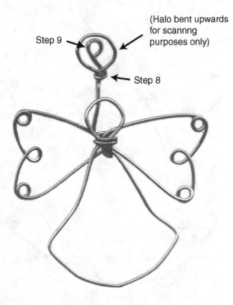

(Halo bent upwards for scannng purposes only)

Step 9

Step 8

(7) Holding the design at the bend with chain nose pliers, wrap the wire around a small dowel or pencil to form the halo.

(8) Finish by looping the wire tail around the neck of the halo to form a circle, and cut the wire (*Figure 3*).

(9) An optional hanging loop can be added prior to cutting the wire (*Figure 3*).

Note: Pegs placed inside the wire designs on this page have been slightly adjusted for illustrative purposes. Please copy the peg placements on the jig template when making this design.

WigJig Olympus Template

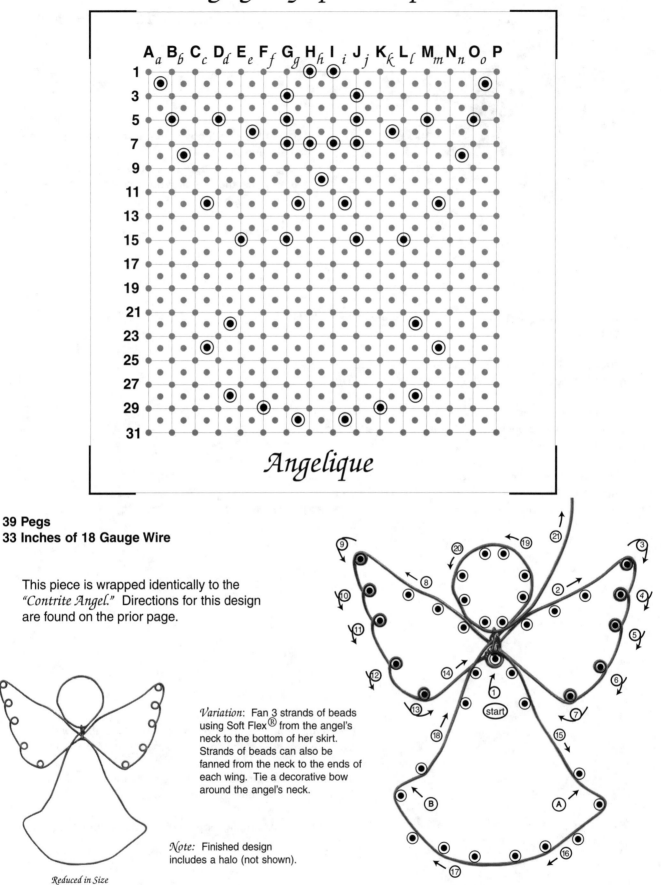

A a **B** b **C** c **D** d **E** e **F** f **G** g **H** h **I** i **J** j **K** k **L** l **M** m **N** n **O** o **P**

Angelique

39 Pegs
33 Inches of 18 Gauge Wire

This piece is wrapped identically to the *"Contrite Angel."* Directions for this design are found on the prior page.

Variation: Fan 3 strands of beads using Soft Flex ® from the angel's neck to the bottom of her skirt. Strands of beads can also be fanned from the neck to the ends of each wing. Tie a decorative bow around the angel's neck.

Note: Finished design includes a halo (not shown).

Reduced in Size

Reduced in Size

WigJig Olympus Template

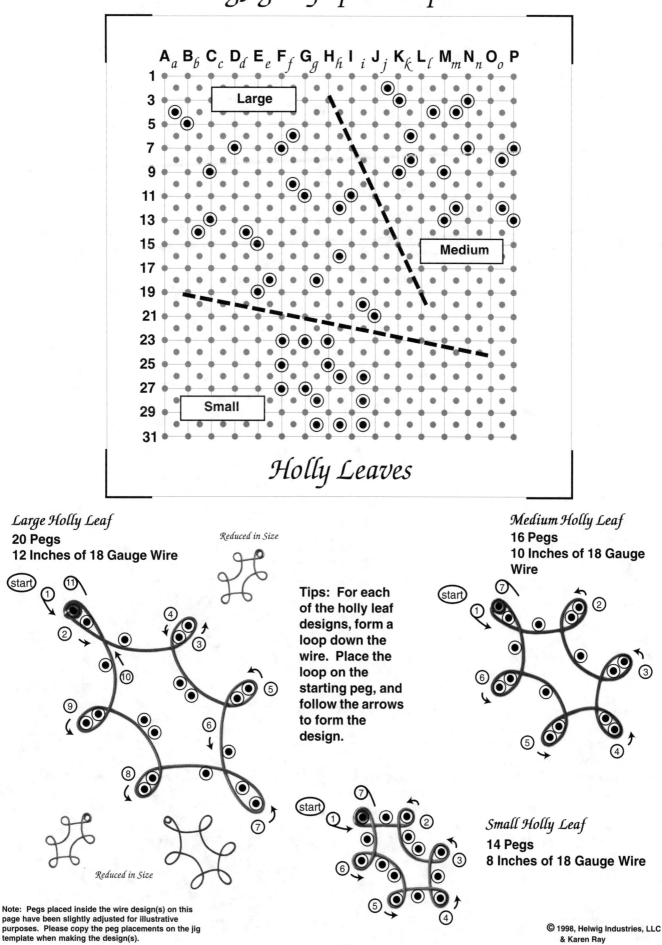

Holly Leaves

Large Holly Leaf
20 Pegs
12 Inches of 18 Gauge Wire

Reduced in Size

Reduced in Size

Tips: For each of the holly leaf designs, form a loop down the wire. Place the loop on the starting peg, and follow the arrows to form the design.

Medium Holly Leaf
16 Pegs
10 Inches of 18 Gauge Wire

Small Holly Leaf
14 Pegs
8 Inches of 18 Gauge Wire

Note: Pegs placed inside the wire design(s) on this page have been slightly adjusted for illustrative purposes. Please copy the peg placements on the jig template when making the design(s).

WigJig Olympus Template

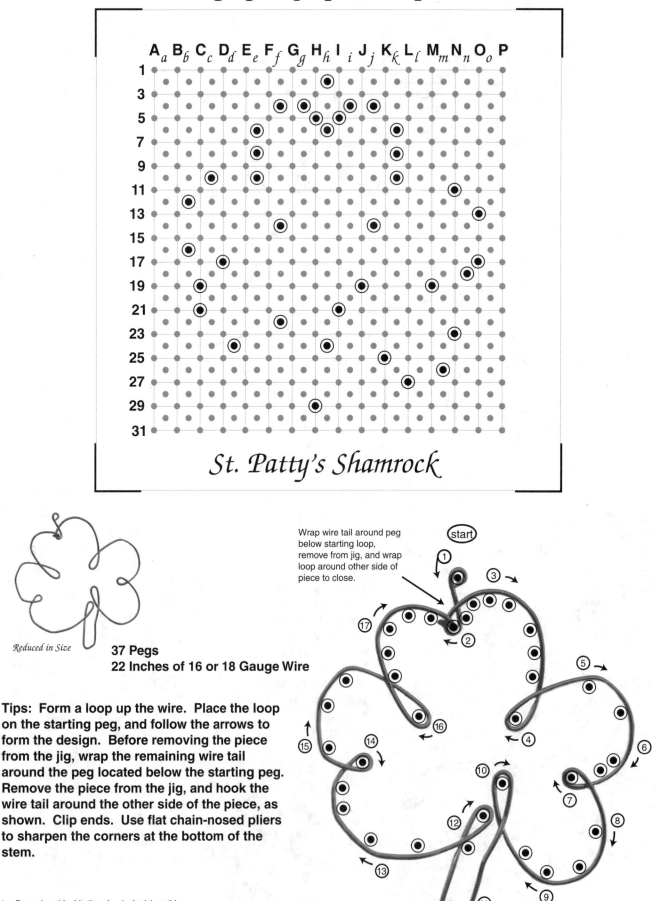

A a B b C c D d E e F f G g H h I i J j K k L l M m N n O o P

1 3 5 7 9 11 13 15 17 19 21 23 25 27 29 31

St. Patty's Shamrock

Reduced in Size

37 Pegs
22 Inches of 16 or 18 Gauge Wire

Tips: Form a loop up the wire. Place the loop on the starting peg, and follow the arrows to form the design. Before removing the piece from the jig, wrap the remaining wire tail around the peg located below the starting peg. Remove the piece from the jig, and hook the wire tail around the other side of the piece, as shown. Clip ends. Use flat chain-nosed pliers to sharpen the corners at the bottom of the stem.

Wrap wire tail around peg below starting loop, remove from jig, and wrap loop around other side of piece to close.

start

Reduced in Size

Note: Pegs placed inside the wire design(s) on this page have been slightly adjusted for illustrative purposes. Please copy the peg placements on the jig template when making the design(s).

© 1998, Helwig Industries, LLC & Karen Ray

142

Wire
Working
Tips &
Hints

(Page intentionally left blank)

Tools and Supplies

The best advice we can provide regarding tools is to purchase the highest quality tools you can afford. Quality pliers that are designed for heavier work are made with a "box joint" to ensure the best alignment. Some are made with a center spring, which keeps the handles of the pliers open as you work. Most pliers are available in two lengths - 4-1/2 inches and 5 inches. It is important that you use the size that fits your hand comfortably, with the pressure evenly distributed to prevent injury or strain. The following discusses the important features of the most popular wire working tools and supplies.

Round Nose Pliers: Round nose pliers have smooth tapered round jaws for making bends, loops, and coils. These pliers are a must for wire working since they are used to form uniform loops. Mark your round nose pliers with a felt-tip marker to ensure that the wire is grasped consistently at the same location throughout a wire working project.

Chain Nose Pliers: Chain nose pliers feature smooth jaws with the nose tapered to a fine point. Quality chain nose pliers have a box joint for lifetime alignment and are used for a variety of techniques. They are important for forming sharp, angular bends in the wire, as well as for grasping wire pieces when making coils and other components.

Bent Chain Nose Pliers: Bent chain nose pliers are similar to chain nose pliers, but with a bend in the nose. This bend facilitates manipulation of the wire in many directions, as well as improving the ability to grasp small areas of wire pieces, such as wrapped eye loops.

Nylon Jaw Pliers: Nylon jaw pliers satisfy three very important requirements. Because the jaws are made of nylon, they do not scratch the soft metal surfaces of the wire, keeping it free from nicks and blemishes. Secondly, they are great for correcting mistakes. In most cases, bent wire can be straightened by drawing the wire length through the jaws. Finally, they can be used very effectively for hardening the wire when hammering or bending the wire back and forth is not the best choice. Placing the wire between the nylon jaws and pressing tightly will often harden the piece. Because the jaws are nylon, they will eventually wear out. However, inexpensive replacement jaws can be purchased from most jewelry supply stores.

Cutters: Sometimes called bead nippers, cutters clip smooth ends in the wire. They are specifically designed to cut flush against the wire, so they are excellent for cutting inside loops to achieve a professional finish to wire designs. (Tip: Before starting to wire wrap, clip the jagged edge left by the prior cut, to save sanding time.)

Bead Stringing Materials: Several of the photographed designs use materials other than wire for stringing beads. Our top recommendation for this application is Soft Flex®. Although it is technically a wire product, it is highly flexible, like string, and can be tied in knots. It is

Tools and Supplies

highly durable and strong (made from many strands of stainless steel), so breakage is virtually eliminated. Integrating Soft Flex® into your wire pieces can add a unique look to your jewelry and ornamental designs. Soft Flex® can be found at bead stores everywhere.

Hammer and Anvil: Hammering adds texture to wire work by flattening and/or marking the wire. It also serves to harden the wire piece for shape retention, particularly when making jewelry pieces that will bear weight. Key tools for hammering include the hammer and an anvil. Hammers can have nylon ends to protect the wire, or can be made of metal. Be certain to use only those hammers designed for jewelry making to ensure professional results. Remember that too much hammering can break the wire, especially at points where metal crosses metal.

Emery Cloth: Emery cloth is used to remove marks, scratches, or burrs. It smooths out the rough edges of wire cuts and gives the work a finished look. Emery cloths can be purchased at your local hardware store. (Tip: Glue emery cloth to small dowels or "frozen bar" sticks to facilitate reaching small areas.)

Files: Files are also an option for removing rough edges and burrs on the ends of wire pieces. Quality files can be purchased at most bead stores. Nail files made specifically for acrylic nails can also be used. Remember that some files are designed to be used in one direction only, and that a sawing motion (back and forth) should be avoided when using these files.

Safety Glasses: Safety glasses come in different styles, and are a necessity to protect your eyes from flying pieces of wire.

WigJigs: Our discussion of tools would not be complete without mentioning our other *WigJigs*. The *Original WigJig* is a 4 peg metal jig used for making clasps and links, 30 of which are found in its companion book, *"The Wonder of Wire"* (see our web site at www.wigjig.com for detailed information).

Tools and Supplies

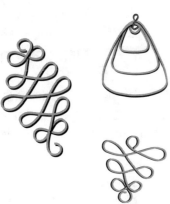

The *Athena WigJig* is a metal jig with 9 stationary pegs, designed specifically to make our signature piece – to the far left. It can also be used to make a variety of wire designs including bracelet links and pendants (see our web site at www.wigjig.com for detailed information).

How to Pick the Right Wire

When choosing wire, five key factors should be considered: size (gauge), type of metal, malleability, shape, and color.

Size (Gauge):

Wire comes in a number of gauges that are measurements of the diameter of the wire. The lower the numerical value of the gauge, the thicker the wire will be. Therefore, 16 gauge wire is significantly thicker than 24 gauge wire. All the designs in this book are made with 16, 18 or 20 gauge wire. The following is a discussion of the various wire gauges and their applicability to designs made on the *Olympus WigJig*. Experimentation will determine which gauge of wire you prefer for a particular design.

18 Gauge: The most versatile wire for use on the *Olympus WigJig* is 18 gauge. It can be used for the majority of designs in this book and works for both large, chunkier designs as well as smaller, more delicate designs. It provides a great look in nearly all types of pieces, ranging from earrings to pendants, yokes, and chains.

16 Gauge: If you are making a large pendant or links that will bear a significant amount of weight such as that of a large bead, then 16 gauge wire is preferable. Be certain to read the section of this chapter entitled *"How to Harden Wire"* for tips on retaining the wire shape of all your pieces. Some designers have had success using 14 gauge wire on the *Olympus WigJig*. This wire is more difficult to bend, however, and should be used after gaining some experience with thinner wires on the jig.

20 Gauge: For delicate pieces, 20 gauge wire may be preferred. However, it is important that little weight, if any, is held by pieces made with 20 gauge wire. Ideal designs for this thinner wire are earrings. Also, ear wires (the piece that passes through a pierced ear) should be made with 20 or 22 gauge wire, since 18 gauge or larger (thicker) will not work for most people. We recommend using no larger wire gauge (thinner) than 20 gauge on the *Olympus WigJig*.

Type of Metal:

Copper: Copper is a great wire to use for practicing your wire working skills. It is inexpensive, yet has a "feel" and bendability comparable to most sterling silver and gold-filled wires. Copper wire can be purchased at bead stores as well as hardware stores. Copper will oxidize or discolor over a period of time – a look preferred by some wire workers. To obtain an immediate patina, purchase Liver of Sulphur at your local bead store. This product will give the copper an antique finish that is quite attractive in casual jewelry pieces.

How to Pick the Right Wire

Brass: Brass is also relatively inexpensive, and will obviously result in a look closer to gold-filled. However, it tarnishes quickly. So again, we generally recommend it for practicing rather than for finished pieces. This wire can also be purchased at most hardware stores.

Silver-Plated or Gold-Plated: Silver-plated or gold-plated wire provides a good start for beginners transitioning from copper to more expensive metals. Because of the plating process, these wires do not have the same look as their more expensive counterparts, (sterling silver and gold–filled). Designs that expose the ends should be avoided when using this wire since the base metal core will be visible. Silver plated and gold plated wire can be purchased at most bead or jewelry supply stores.

Sterling Silver or Gold-Filled: These wire metals are clearly the most popular for making professional-quality jewelry. All gold and silver pieces in our photographs are made with sterling silver or gold-filled wire. These wires are clearly our favorites when making high-quality, designer jewelry pieces, and can be purchased at bead and jewelry supply stores.

Hardness:

Wire hardness is an extremely important factor to consider when purchasing wire. If you choose the wrong hardness, then your wire may be too difficult to bend or too soft to hold its shape. Common types used on the *Olympus WigJig* are "half-hard" and "dead-soft". Standard wire is generally too soft for most applications, so we recommend you experiment with both "dead soft" and "half hard" in 18 or 20 gauge wire. As expected, the "half hard" is stiffer than the "dead soft", and requires more pressure when wire working. For wire working with 16 gauge wire or twisted wire (any gauge), you will likely prefer a "dead soft" wire. With regard to Artistic Wire (colored enamel over a copper core in only one hardness), the 16, 18, and 20 gauge wires all work well on the jig.

Shape:

Wire comes in a variety of cross-section shapes: round, square, half-round, rectangular shank, and bevel. You can even twist your wire to achieve another texture dimension to your designs. (When working with twisted wire, it becomes work-hardened, so it is less malleable than non-twisted wire. Therefore, a softer wire (dead soft) is best when twisting the wire before using it on the jig.)

For the designs in this book, we recommend using round, twisted half-round, or twisted square wire. The variety of designs and textures that can be achieved with these wires can be seen in the photographs in this book.

How to Pick the Right Wire

(Continued)

Color:

Wire color is an important feature to consider when making designs. For fine jewelry pieces, most designers prefer sterling silver or gold-filled. For more casual pieces, copper and brass are frequently used, and in some cases, are oxidized for an antique look.

A great colored wire that we highly recommend is "Artistic Wire," consisting of a copper inner core covered by an enamel coating. It has a great "feel" and malleability, and holds its shape extremely well. In many cases, hardening the wire is not required. It comes in a variety of matte and metallic colors, and can be found in most bead and jewelry supply stores. The versatility of this wire can be seen in the jewelry pieces photographed in this book.

How to Harden the Wire

Hardening the Wire:

Hardening the wire is important to retain the shape of the wire piece, and can be accomplished in a variety of ways. Merely moving or bending the wire will strengthen or harden the wire. This can be accomplished with two pairs of pliers, one on each side of a loop or piece. Moving the wire back and forth several times (6 times maximum), going past center each time will harden the wire design. Bending the wire too far or too many times can result in breakage, so be certain to move the piece back and forth only a few times. Experience and practice will determine the exact number of times required to achieve hardening while avoiding breakage.

The wire can also be hardened by gently pounding the wire piece using a nylon tip hammer, jeweler's block, and/or anvil.

Another wire-hardening technique uses nylon jaw pliers. These pliers allow the user to harden wire pieces without bending or hammering the wire. Pressing the nylon jaws around the piece to harden it into shape is invaluable for many of the pieces in this book. We highly recommend this tool for all wire workers.

Wire Hardening a Figure Eight Component:

Grasp one loop end of a figure eight component. Gently bend the other half of the figure eight to the back from the center and forward past the center approximately 4 times. Be careful to bring the open end back to the center each time so that you do not change the shape of the loop. As the loop is moved back and forth, you can feel the wire harden.

Note: More information on wire hardening can be found in the *"Tools & Supplies"* section of this chapter under *"Hammer and Anvil"* and *"Nylon Jaw Pliers."*

How to Make a Starting Loop *(Basic)*

Wire has a gentle curve when it is removed from the spool. This natural curve is frequently used as an integral part of the wire design. The terms "up the wire" or "down the wire" are used to describe how this curve is incorporated into the design.

Making a Loop Up the Wire

Working *"up the wire"* means bending the wire up and back against its natural curve. When forming a loop, it will bend against the wire's natural curve as shown on the right.

Making a Loop Down the Wire

Working *"down the wire"* means bending the wire into the natural curve, down and under, as shown on the right. When forming a loop, the loop will bend with the natural curve of the wire, and will be a tighter extension of this curve.

How to Start at the Center of the Wire

Measure, then mark the center of the wire. The exact placement of the wire on the jig at the starting location is determined by an "up the wire" or "down the wire" wrap as outlined below.

If the design directions indicate a center start *"up the wire,"* then place the natural curve of the wire on the jig so that the first wrap is against the natural curve of the wire.

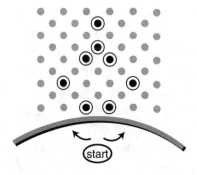

If the design directions indicate a center start *"down the wire,"* then place the wire so that the natural curve of the wire will be in the same general direction as the first wrap.

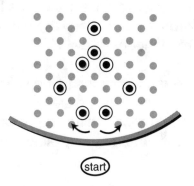

How to Make an Eye Loop

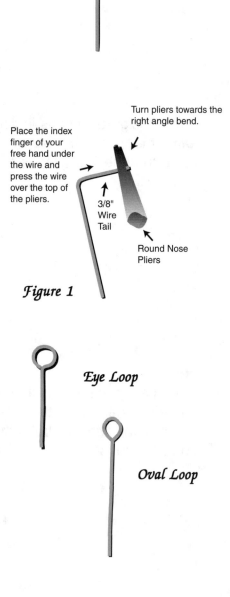

1. Cut a 3 inch piece of 20 gauge wire. With chain nose pliers, grip the wire 3/8 inch from one end and bend this short end against the straight side of the pliers, using a finger on the free hand. This right angle in the wire serves as the center point of the loop and gives the loop a place to sit.

2. Using round nose pliers grasp the end of the 3/8" wire tail approximately one-third of the way down the nose of the pliers. To make an eye loop, hold the 3/8 inch section of the wire in the jaws of the pliers at the very end of the wire so that if you run your finger down the edge of the jaws of the pliers, you cannot feel the wire. To make an oval loop, leave 1/8 inch of wire extending beyond the side of the round nose pliers. Remember, that no matter what the shape, the loop must be closed.

3. While supporting the 3/8 inch section of wire across the index finger of the free hand, pull up as you turn the pliers back towards the bend, and press the wire around the nose of the pliers, forming a perfectly round loop *(Figure 1)*.

4. To reduce stress to the wrist, this loop can be performed in two steps by forming one-half of the loop, repositioning your wrist back to the original position, and completing the loop.

Turn pliers towards the right angle bend.

Place the index finger of your free hand under the wire and press the wire over the top of the pliers.

3/8" Wire Tail

Round Nose Pliers

Figure 1

Eye Loop

Oval Loop

Note: This loop can be used to attach a bead. See the section called *"How to Make a Bead Component Using an Eye Loop or Head Pin"* for details.

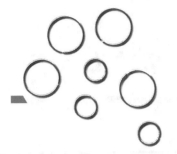

How to Make Jump Rings

1. When using a dowel packaged with the *Original WigJig*, place the wire in the small hole drilled in the dowel. Otherwise, hold the wire tail in place with a finger for stability through the first 3 to 4 wraps around the dowel.

2. Bend the wire around the dowel to form tight circles for the number of jump rings desired.

3. Slide the coil off the dowel. When using the dowel packaged with the *Original WigJig,* cut the wire at the hole before sliding the wire coil off the dowel.

4. Using flush cutters, cut each jump ring one at a time, exactly at the location of the cut of the previous ring (Arrow A). Continue through the entire coil until all rings are formed.

Ⓐ

5. To finish, flatten the two ends of the jump ring together with pliers or blocks. Nylon jaw pliers (see *"Tools and Supplies"* in this chapter) perform this step very well.

6. Before using the jump rings, be certain to harden the wire. See our tips under *"How to Harden Wire"* in this chapter.

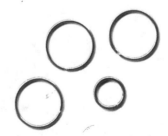

Note: It is easy to make jump rings in any size required. Just change the diameter of the dowel to match the size of the jump ring desired. This is an important skill to learn, particularly for pieces using colored wire for which pre-made jump rings are not available.

How to Make a Figure Eight Loop

1. Cut a piece of 20 gauge wire approximately 12 inches long. This will make several Figure Eight components.

2. Using round nose pliers, place the wire in the pliers one-third of the way down the nose, leaving about 1/16 inch of wire extending beyond the edge of the pliers. While pressing on the wire with the thumb of the free hand, turn the pliers to form the first loop.

3. To reduce stress on the wrist, this step can be performed in two movements. Release the pliers halfway through the turn, and slide them back along the wire about one-quarter of the way. Turn the pliers again to finish forming the first loop.

Note: The black dots indicate the tips of the pliers.

3. Grip the wire just below the loop and make a second loop in the wire by following the directions in step 2.

    As you finish the turn of this second loop, bring the tail of the wire fully around the circle you have formed and across itself to the starting point of this second loop.

4. Cut the wire tail from the completed figure eight by inserting one point of the cutter into the loop just completed, with the two jaws of the cutter sitting on the center crossbar of the figure eight. Cut the wire just as it crosses this center bar.

    Cut wire here, holding cutters at the same angle as the dotted line.

5. As discussed earlier in this chapter, it is important to harden the wire. Grasp one loop end of the figure eight component and gently bend the other half to the back from the center and forward past the center approximately 4 times. Be careful to bring the open end back to the center each time so that the shape of the loop remains unchanged. Do this movement on both halves of the component.

6. Before closing the figure eight on either end, attach the loop to the desired component. Close for the final time.

How to Bind the Wire

1. Cut a 4 inch piece of 22 to 26 gauge wire for each binding wrap. The gauge of the binding wire depends on the size of the wire used in the primary design. Half round wire works well for this type of wrap since the straight side of the half round wire lays flat against the primary wire design.

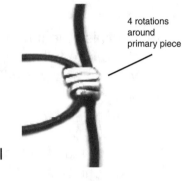

4 rotations around primary piece

2. Using round nose pliers, make a small half loop in the end of the binding wire (down the wire). The half loop should be the size of the wire used to form the primary wire design. (When using half round wire, make certain that the flat side of the wire is on the inside of the loop.)

3. Hook the loop around the back of primary wire design at the binding site. When positioned correctly, the binding wire tail will loop over the front of the primary wire design.

4. Grip the wire tail firmly with chain nose pliers, and wrap the binding wire tightly around the primary design one complete rotation, ending on the back of the primary design.

5. Press the binding wire firmly with chain nose pliers to lock the binding wire into place around the primary design.

6. Grasp the binding wire tail again with chain nose pliers, and wrap tightly around the primary design again (second complete rotation), ending on the back of the primary design. Again, press firmly with chain nose pliers.

7. Repeat a third time to form three tight wraps around the primary design, ending on the back of the piece. Press the wrap firmly with chain nose pliers. Make a minimum of three binding wraps around the primary design (illustrations on this page show 4 rotations). Clip the binding wire tail to complete the wrap.

Note: In order to achieve a neat, professional wrap, it is important to stop at each rotation, and press the wire firmly with the chain nose pliers.

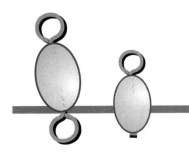

How to Make a Bead Component Using an Eye Loop or Head Pin

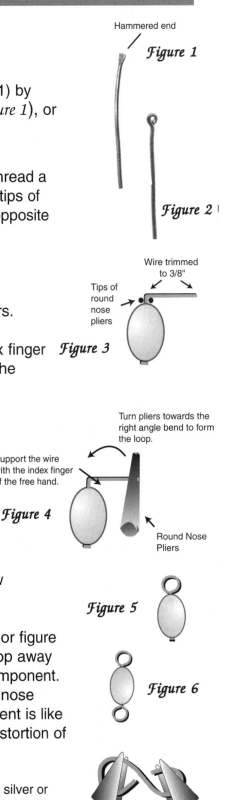

Hammered end

Figure 1

Figure 2

1. Starting with a 3 inch piece of wire, make a head pin, either (1) by flattening 1/8 inch on one end of the wire by hammering (*Figure 1*), or (2) by making a tiny loop at the end of the wire (*Figure 2*). *

2. Thread a bead onto the wire. (If the bead has a large hole, thread a small bead onto the wire first to act as a stopper.) Using the tips of round nose pliers, bend a right angle turn in the wire on the opposite side of the bead from the head pin, as close to the bead as possible. Cut the wire tail to 3/8 inches (*Figure 3*).

   Wire trimmed to 3/8"

   Tips of round nose pliers

3. Using round nose pliers, grasp the end of the 3/8" wire tail approximately one-third of the way down the nose of the pliers.

   Figure 3

4. While supporting the 3/8 inch section of wire across the index finger of the free hand, pull up as you turn the pliers back towards the bend, and press the wire around the nose of the pliers, forming a perfectly round loop (*Figures 4 and 5*). (To reduce stress to the wrist, this loop can be performed in two steps by forming one-half of the loop, repositioning your wrist back to the original position, and completing the loop.)

   Turn pliers towards the right angle bend to form the loop.

   Support the wire with the index finger of the free hand.

   Figure 4

   Round Nose Pliers

5. This same technique can be used to attach a bead within a chain by forming a loop at both ends of the bead. Cut a length of wire 1 inch longer than the bead. Make an eye loop in one end, and center the bead on the wire. Follow steps 3 and 4 to complete the component (*Figure 6*).

   Figure 5

   Figure 6

6. To join this component to another (such as links, jump rings, or figure eight loops), use chain nose pliers to swing the end of the loop away from you only far enough to insert the loop from the other component. After inserting the loop from the other component, use chain nose pliers to swing the open end of the wire closed. This movement is like opening and closing a gate and should be used to prevent distortion of the loop (*Figure 7*).

   * *Note*: Head pins can be purchased at most bead stores (base metal, sterling silver or gold filled).

Figure 7

How to Wrap a Bead

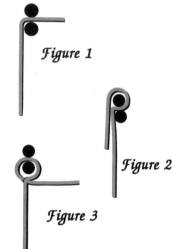

Figure 1

Figure 2

Figure 3

1. Cut a 12 inch piece of 22 gauge wire. This length of wire will wrap several beads. Using round nose pliers, grip the wire 1-1/2 inches from one end, and form a right angle, by bending the wire across the side of the pliers *(Figure 1)*.

2. Moving the jaws of the pliers into the right angle, bend the short wire tail over the top jaw of the pliers, and straight down to the bottom jaw to form a partial loop *(Figure 2)*.

3. Move the pliers so that one jaw is inside this partial loop and the other is on top of the loop. Continue to bend the wire around the bottom jaw of the pliers and complete the loop. The short wire tail will be perpendicular to the long one *(Figure 3)*.

6. Place chain nose pliers across the flat part of this loop, and with the thumb and forefinger of the free hand, wrap the short wire tail around the long wire. Taking care to keep the two pieces of wire perpendicular, wrap two complete turns, and cut the excess from the short wire tail, tucking the cut end so that it will not snag *(Figures 4, 5, and 6)*.

7. Thread a bead onto the long wire. Grasp the wire next to the bead with tips of the pliers. Repeat steps 1 through 6 *(Figure 7)*. (See Marj's tip.) File all ends smooth.

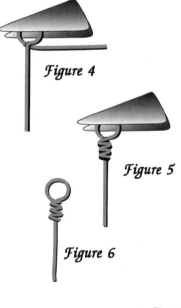

Figure 4

Figure 5

Figure 6

Marj's Tip

Use chain nose pliers to measure the width of the first wrap (Figure 8). Place the pliers at the other end of the bead at the measurement point, and form the right angle for the second bead wrap (Figure 9). The wrap widths at each end of the bead will be identical.

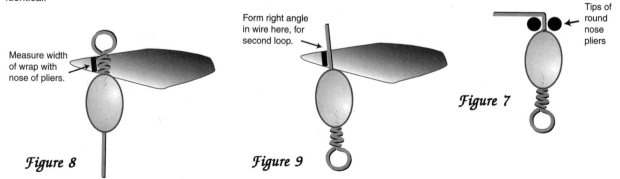

Measure width of wrap with nose of pliers.

Figure 8

Form right angle in wire here, for second loop.

Figure 9

Tips of round nose pliers

Figure 7

How to Double Wrap a Bead

1. Cut a 12 inch piece of 22 gauge wire. This length of wire will wrap several beads. Using round nose pliers, grip the wire 1-1/2 inches from one end. Form a right angle, by bending the wire across the side of the pliers.

2. Moving the jaws of the pliers into the right angle, bend the short wire tail over the top jaw of the pliers, and straight down to the bottom jaw to form a partial loop.

3. Move the pliers so that one jaw is inside this partial loop and the other is on top of the loop. Continue to bend the wire around the bottom jaw of the pliers and complete the loop. The short wire tail will be perpendicular to the long one.

4. Place chain nose pliers across the flat part of this loop and, with the thumb and forefinger of the free hand, wrap the short wire tail around the long wire. Taking care to keep the two pieces of wire perpendicular, wrap one complete turn and cut the excess from the short wire tail, tucking the cut end around the primary wire to prevent snagging.

Note: The black dots indicate the tips of the pliers.

How to Double Wrap a Bead

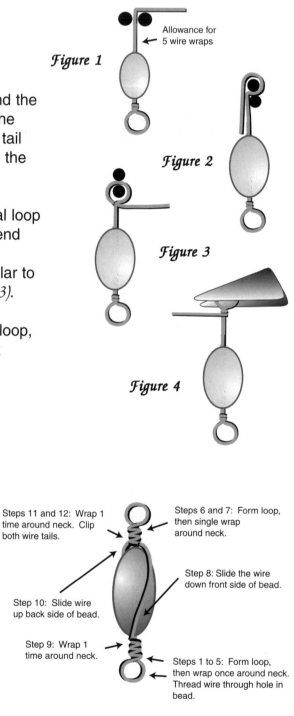

5. Thread a bead onto the wire.

6. Leaving adequate allowance for 3 wire wraps, bend the wire at a right angle *(Figure 1)*. Move the jaws of the pliers into the right angle, and bend the short wire tail over the top jaw of the pliers, and straight down to the bottom jaw to form a partial loop *(Figure 2)*.

   Move the pliers so that one jaw is inside this partial loop and the other is on top of the loop. Continue to bend the wire around the bottom jaw of the pliers, and complete the loop. The wire tail will be perpendicular to the wire that is threaded through the bead *(Figure 3)*.

7. Place chain nose pliers across the flat part of this loop, and wrap the short wire around the long wire neck once, taking care to keep the two wire pieces perpendicular to each other *(Figure 4)*.

8. After the first wrap, slide the wire across the front of the bead to the other end of the bead (first loop that was formed) *(Figure 5)*.

9. Wrap the wire around the neck of the first loop one time *(Figure 5)*.

10. Slide the wire across the back of the bead (opposite side of step 8) to the other loop (second loop that was formed) *(Figure 5)*.

11. Wrap the wire around the neck of the second loop one time *(Figure 5)*.

12. Clip, then tuck wire tail around the primary wire (wire passing through the bead) to prevent snagging. File all ends smooth.

Figure 1

Figure 2

Figure 3

Figure 4

Allowance for 5 wire wraps

Steps 11 and 12: Wrap 1 time around neck. Clip both wire tails.

Steps 6 and 7: Form loop, then single wrap around neck.

Step 8: Slide the wire down front side of bead.

Step 10: Slide wire up back side of bead.

Step 9: Wrap 1 time around neck.

Steps 1 to 5: Form loop, then wrap once around neck. Thread wire through hole in bead.

Figure 5

How to Make a Coil or Scroll

1. Cut a 9-1/2 inch piece of 18 gauge wire.

2. Measure, then mark the center of the wire with a felt-tip marker. Place two additional marks 3/4 inch on each side of the center mark.

3. Using round nose pliers, make a loop down the wire. On the other end of the wire, working up the wire, make a second small loop. If the coils/scrolls will be joined to other wire components, be certain that the centers of the coils/scrolls are adequately sized to allow the connecting wire to pass through.

4. Using bent chain nose pliers, hold the wire across the flat part of the loop. Allow all of the wire tail and a bit of the loop to extend beyond the side of the pliers. Using the thumb of the free hand, gently press the wire toward the pliers. Open the pliers and rotate the loop, keeping the same amount of the loop inside the pliers at all times (this ensures consistency in the tightness of the wrap). Gently press the wire again toward the pliers. Continue to wrap until the 3/4 inch mark is reached.

5. Repeat step 4 to form the second coil/scroll at the other end of the wire. Continue to coil until the two ends meet. Even the coils/scrolls.

Notes: For coils, make tight wraps that lie next to each other. For scrolls, wrap more loosely. The size of the coil/scroll is determined by the length and the gauge of the wire. Wire lengths required for each coil/scroll can vary from 4 inches to 12 inches. Recommended minimum allowances per scroll/coil are: 4 inches of 16 gauge wire, 3 inches of 18 gauge wire, and 2 inches of 20 gauge wire. For tips on making symmetrical coils, see *"How to Make a Double Swirl."*

Some scrolls can be made on the *Olympus WigJig*. See *"Swirly S-Links"* in the *"Chains, Links & Clasps"* chapter for directions.

How to Make an "S" Swirl

1. Using round nose pliers, make a loop down the wire. On the other end of the wire, working up the wire, make a second small loop. If the coils/scrolls will be joined to other wire components, be certain that the centers of the coils/scrolls are adequately sized to allow the wire to pass through.

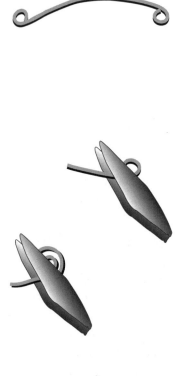

2. Using bent chain nose pliers, place one of the entire loops plus 1/8 inch of the wire tail flat inside the pliers. Using the thumb of the free hand, gently press the wire toward the pliers. Open the pliers and rotate the loop, keeping the whole loop and 1/8 inch of the wire tail inside the pliers. Gently press the wire again toward the pliers. How much of the tail you leave inside the pliers with each rotation will determine how tight or how open the coil/scroll will be.

3. Make a coil/scroll at the other end of the wire, using the same technique. The piece can be varied by changing the number of turns per coil/scroll. Additionally, as shown in the drawings below, the tightness of the coil/scroll can also be varied.

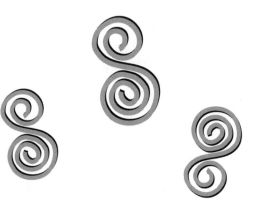

How to Make a Double Swirl

1. Cut a 4 inch piece of 20 gauge wire. Measure and mark the center of the wire with a felt-tip marker. Place two additional marks 3/4 inch on each side of the center mark.

2. Using round nose pliers, make two loops down the wire at each end. If the coils/scrolls will be joined to other wire components, be certain that the centers of the coils/scrolls are adequately sized to allow the wire to pass through.

3. Using bent chain nose pliers, place one of the loops flat inside the pliers, allowing all of the wire tail and a bit of the loop to extend beyond the edge of the pliers. Using the thumb of the free hand, gently press the wire toward the pliers to form a tight coil. Open the pliers and rotate the loop, keeping the all of the wire tail and a bit of the loop outside the pliers. Gently press the wire again toward the pliers, continuing to form a tight coil. Continue to wrap the coil until you reach the 3/4 inch mark.

4. Repeat step 3 using the other end of the wire to make the second coil.

5. Using a mandrel (dowel, pen, round nose pliers, or knitting needle), bend the wire at the center mark to form a hairpin turn. Check to see that both ends of the wire are evenly coiled. Adjust, as required.

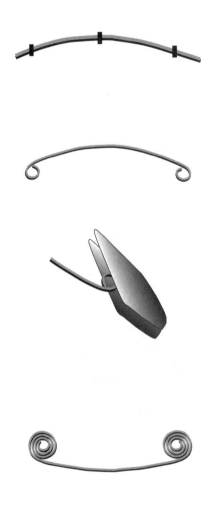

How to Make a Double Swirl

This design can be used to form a hook and eye for bracelets or necklaces.

To form the hook, place the Double Swirl design between the jaws of round nose pliers *(Figure 1)*, and fold the hairpin portion of the piece over on top of the coils *(Figure 2)*.

Figure 1

Grip wire between nose of pliers here.

Figure 2

To form the eye, start with the basic piece, and cross the two flat coils over each other to form a single-strand eye (coils will rest directly on top of each other) or a double-strand eye (coils will cross beyond each other).

To ensure coils and scrolls are symmetrical, carefully look at one of the coils, note its exact orientation, then count the number of turns. To count the second coil, hold it in the exact "mirror image" orientation, and count the number of turns, using the identical starting and stopping points for the first count.

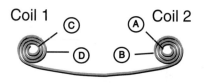

Coil 1   Coil 2

Count from A to B for the first coil and from C to D for the second coil. Point C is the mirror image of point A, and point B is the mirror image of point D.

How to Cap a Bead with a Coil

1. Cut a 9-1/2 inch piece of 18 gauge wire.

2. Measure and mark the center of the wire. Place two additional marks 3/4 inch on each side of the center mark.

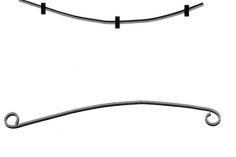

3. Using round nose pliers, make a loop down the wire. On the other end of the wire, working up the wire, make a second small loop. Be certain that the centers of the coils/scrolls are adequately sized to allow wire to pass through.

4. Using bent chain nose pliers, hold the wire across the flat part of the loop. Allow all of the wire tail and a bit of the loop to extend beyond the side of the pliers. Using the thumb of the free hand, gently press the wire toward the pliers. Open the pliers and rotate the loop, keeping the same amount of the loop inside the pliers at all times (this ensures consistency in the tightness of the wrap). Gently press the wire again toward the pliers. Continue to wrap until the 3/4 inch mark is reached.

5. Repeat step 4 to form the second coil/scroll at the other end of the wire. Continue to coil until the 2 coiled/scrolled ends meet. Even the coils/scrolls.

6. Holding the coils so that the wrap looks like the letter "S," gently fold one side over the other, like closing a book.

How to Cap a Bead with a Coil

7. Using bent chain nose pliers, gently push out the ends. Press the center of the cage gently apart and insert the bead. Work the wire around the bead so that the ends are symmetric.

8. To make the wrap shown to the right, (ends tightly wrapped and center loosely wrapped around a long bead or large round bead), gently work the wire into the desired shape manually.

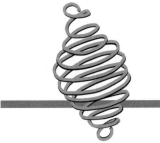

How to Make a Coil Cage

1. Cut a 9-1/2 inch piece of 18 gauge wire.

2. Measure and mark the center of the wire. Place two additional marks 3/4 inch on each side of the center mark.

3. Using round nose pliers, make two loops down the wire at each end. If the coils/scrolls will be joined to other wire components, be certain that the centers of the coils/scrolls are adequately sized to allow the wire to pass through.

4. Using bent chain nose pliers, hold the wire across the flat part of the loop. Allow all of the wire tail and a bit of the loop to extend beyond the side of the pliers. Using the thumb of the free hand, gently press the wire toward the pliers. Open the pliers and rotate the loop, keeping the same amount of the loop inside the pliers at all times (this ensures consistency in the tightness of the wrap). Gently press the wire again toward the pliers. Continue to wrap until the 3/4 inch mark is reached.

5. Repeat step 4 to form the second coil at the other end of the wire.

6. Continue to wrap the coils until one slides over the other.

7. Using bent chain nose pliers, push out the centers of the coils slightly and then gently tug on the ends with your fingers to open the coil. Separate each coil evenly by gently sliding a small ruler around and through each coil.

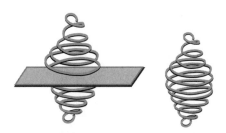

How to Wrap a Bead in a Coil Cage

1. Make the coiled cage by following steps 1 through 7 under *"How to Make a Coil Cage."* Using bent chain nose pliers, push out the center of each coil slightly, and pull out the ends to open the coil, keeping the spacing even.

3. Insert a bead or a stone in the cage by spreading the wire gently at the center and placing bead inside. Close and even up wires of the cage,

4. To finish the cage leaving the bead loose, turn the wire ends out at each end of the cage and form hanging loops using round nose pliers.

5. To finish the cage with the bead(s) threaded onto a wire, cut a piece of wire (the full length of the bead(s) plus 1-1/2 inches). Make a loop in one end of the wire, thread the wire tail through the top hole of the cage, through the center of the bead(s), and finally, through the bottom hole of the cage. Form a loop on the end to complete.

Notes: The length and gauge of the wire determines the size of the cage. Most cages are made with 4 to 12 inches of wire. Label each practice cage with wire length and gauge size to keep for future reference.

How to Make a Pin Using the Jig

1. To adapt a wire design to a pin using the *Olympus WigJig*, be certain both the starting and ending loops are double-wrapped. To start, make a double loop using round nose pliers, and place this on the first peg. For the ending loop, be certain to wrap 2-3/4 times (so the wire tail comes back across the piece correctly). Use the long pegs for both the starting and ending loops.

2. *Figure 1* shows the wire piece as it looks on the jig, including the double wraps around both the starting and ending pegs.

   In *Figure 2*, the double wrapped loops have been spread apart for illustrative purposes only. This should not be done when actually making the pin.

3. After removing the piece from the jig, bend the starting and ending loops 90 degrees forward (*Figure 3*, arrows A and B).

4. To finish, open the bottom loop on the back of the pin to form the hook. File the wire tail to a sharp point. File end of hook to round and smooth.

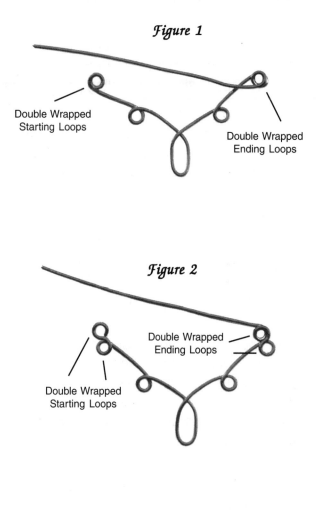

Figure 1

Double Wrapped Starting Loops

Double Wrapped Ending Loops

Figure 2

Double Wrapped Ending Loops

Double Wrapped Starting Loops

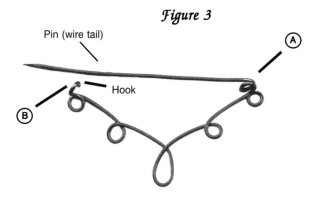

Figure 3

Pin (wire tail)

Hook

Ⓐ

Ⓑ

How to Make a Pin Without the Jig

1. Form a starting loop 1/2 inch down the wire. This wire tail will form the "hook" for the pin. The other wire tail that remains after the design is wrapped will serve as the "pin." Place the starting loop on the jig, and wrap the pin as originally designed (no extra wraps around the starting and ending pegs as discussed on the prior page). Remove the wire piece from the jig.

2. To make the pin, place the piece face down with the back facing you. Bend the long wire tail at a 90 degree angle upward and away from the wire piece. In other words, with the back of the wire piece facing you, the long wire tail will be pointing directly at you.

3. Place round nose pliers 1/8 inch down the wire from the 90 degree bend formed in step 2 (the bend should be on the same side of the pliers as the wrapped piece). Wrap the wire 1-1/4 times (450 degrees) around the nose of the pliers. The wrap should be completed so that the wire tail forms the "pin" in the appropriate location relative to the completed wire piece.

4. The hook for the pin should be formed at the opposite end of the piece from the wire tail. Bend the wire 90 degrees from the plane of the piece. In other words, if the back of the piece is facing towards you, the short wire tail should be pointing upward and directly at you. Place round nose pliers 1/8 inch from the bend (the bend should be on the same side of the pliers as the wrapped piece), and make a loop around the pliers. Snip the end to form the open hook.

5. To finish, file the end of the wire hook to smooth and round. File the end of the pin to a sharp point.